The Decision To Relocate the Japanese Americans

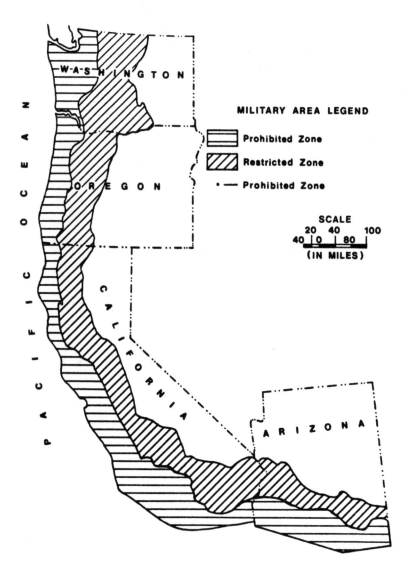

MILITARY AREA LEGEND

▭ Prohibited Zone

▨ Restricted Zone

•— Prohibited Zone

SCALE

20 40   100
40 | 0 | 80 |
(IN MILES)

This map shows the area from which Japanese Americans were relocated. The shaded areas represent the original "Military Area No. 1," which was originally divided into "prohibited" and "restricted" zones. Eventually, the zones and areas became meaningless, as all Japanese, citizens and aliens, in the four states were incarcerated.

Roger Daniels

State University of New York, Fredonia

The America's Alternatives Series

Edited by Harold M. Hyman

The Decision to Relocate the Japanese Americans

J. B. Lippincott Company
Philadelphia/New York/Toronto

ISBN 0-397-47326-5
Library of Congress Catalog Card Number 74-28362
Printed in the United States of America

1 3 5 7 9 8 6 4 2

Library of Congress Cataloging in Publication Data

Daniels, Roger.
   The decision to relocate the Japanese Americans.

   (The America's alternatives series)
   Bibliography: p.
   1. Japanese Americans—Evacuation and relocation,
1942-1945. I. Title.
D769.8.A6D36   940.54'72'73   74-28362
ISBN 0-397-47326-5

For my son
Richard John Daniels

Contents

Foreword

"When you judge decisions, you have to judge them in the light of what there was available to do it," noted Secretary of State George C. Marshall to the Senate Committees on the Armed Services and Foreign Relations in May 1951.[1] In this spirit, each volume in the "America's Alternatives" series examines the past for insights which History—perhaps only History—is peculiarly fitted to offer. In each volume the author seeks to learn why decision-makers in crucial public policy or, more rarely, private choice situations adopted a course and rejected others. Within this context of choices, the author may ask what influence then-existing expert opinion, administrative structures, and budgetary factors exerted in shaping decisions? What weights did constitutions or traditions have? What did men hope for or fear? On what information did they base their decisions? Once a decision was made, how was the decision maker able to enforce it? What attitudes prevailed toward nationality, race, region, religion, or sex, and how did these attitudes modify results?

We freely ask such questions of the events of our time. This "America's Alternatives" volume transfers appropriate versions of such queries to the past.

In examining those elements that were a part of a crucial historical decision, the author has refrained from making judgments based upon attitudes, information, or values that were not current at the time the decision was made. Instead, as much as possible he or she has explored the past in terms of data and prejudices known to persons contemporary to the event.

1. U.S. Senate, Hearings Before the Committees on the Armed Services and the Foreign Relations of the United States, *The Military Situation in the Far East* (82 Cong., 2d sess.), Part I, p. 382. Professor Ernest R. May's "Alternatives" volume directed me to this source and quotation.

Nevertheless, the following reconstruction of one of America's major alternative choices speaks implicitly and frequently, explicitly to present concerns.

In form, this volume consists of a narrative and analytical historical essay (Part One), within which the author has identified by use of headnotes (i.e., *Alternative 1*, etc.) the choices which he believes were actually before the decision makers with whom he is concerned.

Part Two of this volume contains, in whole or part, the most appropriate source documents that illustrate the Part One Alternatives. The Part Two Documents and Part One essay are keyed for convenient use (i.e., references in Part One will direct readers to appropriate Part Two Documents). The volume's Part Three offers users further guidance in the form of a Bibliographic Note.

Americans' whole-hearted participation in World War II left a home front record marked by unity and consensus, compared to the Civil War and the First World War. The harsh exception to the fact of World War II unity was the decision in West Coast states and in Washington by civilian and military leaders of states and nation, after the stunning Japanese victory at Pearl Harbor, to render helpless by forced relocations into prison-like camps, the many thousands of residents of Japanese descent.

Historians, political scientists, and sociologists have labored long and well in the intervening thirty years to explain the relocation decision and its effects. Professor Roger Daniels has been one of the preeminent historical analysts of these unhappy events. In this volume he reviews, in part from newly available sources, the question of the need and responsibility for the distrust of the West Coast's Japanese residents and the consequent relocation. His analysis and documents allow the most insightful glimpses yet available into the perceptions that shaped a fateful policy.

Harold M. Hyman
Rice University

Preface

The personal and intellectual debts that one incurs in a life of scholarship can never be fully acknowledged in a brief statement since teachers, colleagues, students, and friends all help shape one's view of the world. I have, in the past dozen years, talked to literally thousands of people—oppressors, victims, and observers—about the relocation experience. There is no adequate way to acknowledge them other than to say that I almost always received more than I gave. The contributions of other scholars in the field are acknowledged in the Notes and in the Bibliographic Note.

Historians live on the labors of librarians and archivists. Of particular assistance in the creation of this work were John Saulitis and his staff at the State University of New York, Fredonia, James E. O'Neill, Director, Franklin D. Roosevelt Library, Hyde Park, and Thomas E. Hohnmann of the National Archives who supervised the microfilming of most of the unpublished documents used in Part Two.

I have known the general editor of this series, Harold M. Hyman, for nearly two decades as teacher, colleague and friend. In all of these roles I have found him knowing, energetic and exuberant, so it came as no surprise to discover that he was also an editor of precision, tact and ingenuity. Without his work, this book would be less than it is.

Mrs. Mary Notaro, who is the soul of the Fredonia History Department, typed the manuscript with the skill, speed, and graciousness that is so typical of her.

And last, but by no means least, I must again thank my wife, Judith, who, as always, has improved my grammar and excised many of my indiscretions. Despite all this help my name alone appears on the title page so I must take full responsibility for any errors of commission or omission.

Roger Daniels
State University of New York, Fredonia

Part One

The Decision to Relocate the Japanese Americans

1

The Perception of a Threat

Historians of freedom in the United States have often remarked, with pleasure and sometimes pride, that relatively speaking, there were many fewer violations of civil liberties during World War II than during World War I. One index to this phenomenon is the number of federal indictments under federal security statutes: just twenty-six during the second war as opposed to more than twenty-five hundred during the first. These historians usually point out that there was a major exception: the wartime incarceration of the West Coast Japanese Americans. Writing in 1959, Harold M. Hyman called it "the major blot" on an otherwise improved record. He then noted that, as opposed to earlier violations, "even this sorry event was handled by officials rather than by vigilantes. Loyalty-testing in World War II remained from 1941 through 1945 . . . in the hands of the executive departments of the national government."[1]

Given our past history of vigilantism, of local zeal outstripping federal restraint, this was a reasonable view. By the 1970s, however, it was possible to have a different perspective. The years since World War II have spawned loyalty-security programs of a magnitude entirely without precedent in American life. Government snooping, sometimes using ultrasophisticated technological equipment, sometimes merely legitimizing shabby gossip, has grown to previously undreamed of proportions. When conservative Senator Sam J. Ervin, Jr., of North Carolina becomes concerned about the level, intensity and legitimacy of federal loyalty-security programs, matters have obviously become pretty bad. Viewed in this light, the World War II civil liberties record takes on a different significance. It is possible to argue that the massive violation of the civil liberties of one group, the West Coast Japanese, was an ominous prefiguration of the future in which an increasingly powerful federal bureaucracy would exercise more and more surveillance and potential control over groups and individuals deemed, in one way or another, to be deviant. Mass surveillance and mass arrests have occurred; mass incarceration, however, has not yet recurred. The Japanese American experience thus remains, happily, a unique experience. As such, it merits much study and reflection. In a previous work, I examined this sad complex of events essentially from the point of the view of the victims, the men, women and children who were shipped off to ten jerry-built concentration camps located in some of the least hospitable parts of the interior of our continent.[2] In the present work I am concerned almost exclusively with the decision-making process by which this legal atrocity came about.

The Background For Fear

One of the constant problems for a historian is where to start his story. Rather than retell the Japanese American tale before the onset of World War II, let us begin in 1940. According to the census taken in that year, there were 126,947 Japanese living in the continental United States, more than sixty percent of them native-born citizens. Nearly nine out of ten lived in one of the three Pacific Coast states, with nearly three-quarters of the total inside the borders of California. Demographically, because of changes made in American immigration regulations in the early twentieth century, the Japanese American community had an unusual structure. The first generation of immigrants, or Issei*, was past the prime of life. Most Issei males were between fifty and sixty-four years of age; their wives were between forty and fifty-four. The major group of their children, the Nisei, was between twenty and twenty-four years of age. If one constructs a graph of the available demographic data it is seen that there was a "missing" generation of Japanese Americans, which, under "normal" conditions would have been born in the years 1905-1915, when very few Japanese women had come to the United States. If one constructs a "typical" Japanese American family, children were born in the years 1918-1922 to a thirty-five year old father and a twenty-five year old mother. Under most circumstances, the absence of this generation would exacerbate tensions between Issei father and Nisei son. American law made this tension even more serious. With the exception of a handful of males who were naturalized as a result of service in the United States armed forces during World War I, the nearly fifty thousand Issei adults were all "aliens ineligible to citizenship," and, with the outbreak of war, enemy aliens.

Although by all the normal indices of social deviancy—crime, delinquency, broken homes, institutionalization, etc.—the Japanese Americans were model members of society, they were viewed with fear, suspicion, and loathing by most other Americans. The reasons for this are of course complex, like any other pathological reaction, but the essential cause is clear: their skins were yellow. In addition, unlike their fellow Asians, the Chinese, they were then perceived as a threat, both internally and externally. Within the United States Japanese Americans were concentrated economically in high-yield, labor-intensive agricultural and horticultural pursuits. Externally, their homeland, Japan, was seen, not without reason, as a possible threat, not only to the United States, but also to what a popular publicist of the 1920s has called "white world supremacy." It was this unique combination of factors— American racism, the upward mobility of Japanese Americans, their geographical concentration, and the external threat posed by Japanese

---

*Immigrants from Japan are called "Issei," from the combination of Japanese words for "one" and "generation"; their native born children of the second generation are called "Nisei"; third, fourth and fifth generations are called "Sansei," "Yonsei" and "Gosei." A special term, "Kibei," is used to describe Nisei who were sent to Japan for a significant part of their education.

militarism—which created the essential preconditions for the relocation decisions. The mere existence of these preconditions, however, did not automatically produce the decision for relocation. Other preconditions existed which tended to mitigate against such a step. These included a growing national concern for civil liberty, the liberal nature of the national administration, and the American tradition of minimal action at the national level concerning internal security.

Beginning Preparations Against "The Enemy"

After the outbreak of World War II, and especially after the fall of Norway, the low countries, and France in the first half of 1940, the probability of direct American involvement in World War II increased. At the same time, federal officials began to attempt to study the "lessons," real and imagined, of our experience in World War I and what was then thought to be happening in Europe, as part of our preparation for war. On May 22, 1940, President Franklin D. Roosevelt, in a message to Congress, referred to the "startling sequence of international events" and used this as a rationale for recommending the transfer of the Immigration and Naturalization Service from the Labor Department to the Department of Justice. The next month the Alien Registration Act was passed, which required every alien in the United States to register with federal authorities every year. In one sense this latter act was a kind of protection for aliens from harassment by state and local authorities, since the presence of federal legislation preempted local action. Although the attorney general of the United States insisted that "no stigma" was attached to registration, nevertheless the coupling of the two events—transfer of control over immigrants from the essentially protective Labor Department to the essentially punitive Department of Justice, and the unprecedented registration requirement (which in 1975 is still in effect) can be taken as an indication that there were forces within the federal government intent upon introducing some of the traditional trappings of authoritarian government. (The same Congress also passed the Smith Act, the first peacetime sedition law since the short-lived Alien and Sedition Act of the John Adams administration.)

The thirteen months between the reelection of Franklin Delano Roosevelt for an unprecedented third term in 1940 and the attack on Pearl Harbor in December, 1941, saw no new significant anti-alien or internal security legislation. During that time events in Europe occupied most of the national attention, and American attitudes toward the war changed essentially from a question of "whether" the United States would become involved to a question of "when" that involvement would occur. Yet, in retrospect, it is now possible to discover that certain steps had been taken against Japanese residents in this country. *(Alternative 1: Civilian Primacy in Domestic Internal Security.)* In the week of the German invasion of Poland, President Roosevelt had placed the Federal Bureau of Investigation in sole charge of internal security and antisubversion matters. It was a major expansion of the role of the bureau and its chief, J. Edgar Hoover. Much of the administration's emphasis—and the emphasis of later historians—has been on the way in which this federalization of antisubversive activities mitigated against state and local vigilantism. As Attorney General Robert H. Jackson put it to an August, 1940 conference of state governors and law enforcement officials:

> The detection of spies is no job for merely well-meaning citizens, however patriotic. The foreign agent and the skilled spy are trained to their jobs and can be dealt with only by one who is trained to his job. Amateur efforts or mob efforts almost invariably seize upon people who are merely queer or who hold opinions of an unpopular tinge, or who talk too much or otherwise give offense.[3]

Yet despite these precautions, which were in themselves a mixed blessing at best, amateur opinion would prevail over the professional in the matter of the Japanese Americans. Pressures from state politicians would prevail over the protest of the Justice Department's professionals, and the urgings of an undistinguished theater commander, prompted by a few lawyers in uniform, would prevail over the advice of the General Staff of the army. Had maximization of civil liberty, rather than mere professionalism, been the administration's goal, a different result might have ensued.

Left to their own devices, the professionals did not do so badly. Although it is not yet possible for historians to examine the investigative records of the Federal Bureau of Investigation, its prewar procedure can be inferred from its immediate post-Pearl Harbor actions. Since no indictments for espionage or sabotage were ever sought against any Japanese resident in the United States, we must assume that the FBI found no such evidence. It did find a number of organizations within the Japanese American community which had direct and indirect ties with the Japanese government, and it operated on the assumption that the officers of these organizations were therefore suspect. These organizations were largely business, cultural, and religious in nature. The most notorious of these, before and after Pearl Harbor, was the Society of the Amur River, a Japanese organization originally aimed at the encouraging of Japanese settlement and conquest of Manchuria. By the 1930s, the society generally supported Japanese imperialism. Its function in the Japanese American community was to garner financial and moral support for Japanese interests. The fact that the Japanese characters for "Amur River" also mean "Black Dragon"—obviously reflecting the river's color, course, and strength—made it possible to call the group "The Black Dragon Society," which has a sinister ring to American ears attuned to wily oriental exponents of the yellow peril.

The leaders of these groups were almost universally somewhat elderly, inoffensive gentlemen. Yet the FBI officially concluded that the officers of these groups were subversive, and placed their names on a master list or lists to be used in case of war between the United States and Japan. Having done that, the FBI consistently, but not vehemently, opposed further actions against Japanese Americans. One suspects that a major reason for this restraint was that any further action was, at least by implication, a criticism of the bureau, and, as is well known, J. Edgar Hoover, to his dying day, was hypersensitive to any criticism. Whatever the reasons, before war came, the Department of Justice was committed to a policy of relative restraint which would have incarcerated a small number of Japanese aliens resident in the United States. Since, by prevailing concepts of international conduct, the incarceration of enemy aliens in wartime does not involve a trial, no question of guilt or innocence for those on the list arose, but there was, at least, associational evidence against everyone on the list.

The military departments of the executive branch, not yet unified into a Department of Defense, also prepared to deal with enemy aliens. In July, 1940, Army Intelligence took the position that past American practice did "not contemplate sufficiently the importance of military control to counter 'Fifth Column' activities. These activities have been so successful in the European War and are so closely integrated with the armed and uniformed forces of the enemy as to force recognition of an internal as well as an external military front. This means that the military will . . . have to provide for the arrest and temporary holding of a large number of suspects."

Because of this position taken by Army Intelligence, the Judge Advocate General was asked in a formal memorandum the next month, the following questions:

a. In the zone of the interior, as differentiated by the theater of operations under military control, to what extent can the military legally, actually control through the Provost Marshal Generals, local forces, police or constabulary, any operations against 'Fifth Columnists'?

b. Can the Military in the zone of the interior participate in the arrest and temporary holding of civilians who are not alien enemies of the United States?

The then Judge Advocate General, Major General Allen W. Gullion, answered in a formal memorandum in mid-August. In response to the first question, he pointed out that control of enemy aliens in wartime, derived from a World War I statute still on the books, called for their arrest "at the pleasure of the President" and defined enemy aliens as males fourteen years of age or older. He also pointed out that the statutes "contemplate their enforcement by civil courts." With respect to the more sinister question "b," which despite its circumlocution clearly anticipated military seizure without trial of civilian citizens, the judge advocate replied in the negative. He held that the military did not have the right even to participate in such arrests except in cases of espionage on military premises or in cases in which martial law was declared.[4]

I can discover no evidence that army planning for wartime control of civilian citizens proceeded any farther than this in the period between the summer of 1940 and Pearl Harbor. In that sixteen-month period the records show that what little concern there was about the interning of civilians revolved mostly about a traditional target group—alien merchant seamen. It is significant, however, that, at its highest staff levels, the army did secretly contemplate exercising police authority over civilian citizens within the continental United States.

The United States Navy did not, apparently, involve itself in any systematic planning concerning aliens, but it had a long-standing concern about a Pacific war—Japan had been our "most probable" naval enemy during most of the twentieth century—and was disturbed that some of its key installations on the West Coast were in close proximity to Japanese settlements, the most significant of which were Bainbridge Island, Washington and Terminal Island, California. The navy also acquired, in the summer of 1940, a new civilian head, Chicago newspaper publisher Frank Knox. Perhaps under the influence of his admirals, Knox became the most vehement proponent of anti-Japanese American measures in Roosevelt's cabinet.

Concern Outside the Military: Congress and the President

In the Congress, too, prewar concern about Japanese Americans was often expressed. Historically, Congress had been much more willing to indulge in anti-Oriental legislation and activity than the executive branch. The exclusion of Chinese in the nineteenth century and the effective exclusion of Japanese in the twentieth had each been forced on a reluctant executive by an adamant Congress. In the years before Pearl Harbor the bulk of anti-Japanese activity in Congress was instigated by Martin Dies, Jr., Democratic congressman from Texas, an anti-New Dealer who was chairman of the House Committee on UnAmerican Activities. Although none of his "investigations" produced anything significant, he would help, in the weeks after Pearl Harbor—and in fact during most of the war—to stir up anti-Japanese sentiment.

Uneasiness about the Japanese was not restricted to demagogues. In August, 1941, a normally responsible New Dealer, John D. Dingell, a Democrat from Michigan, wrote a personal letter to the president suggesting that, if Japan should take any steps against the few American civilians in Japan, the United States could retaliate by causing "the forceful detention or imprisonment in a concentration camp of ten thousand alien Japanese in Hawaii." He also urged that the "one hundred and fifty thousand additional alien Japanese in the United States [be] held in a reprisal reserve."[5] Congressman Dingell's figures do not really make sense—his total of 160,000 approximates the total Japanese American population of Hawaii, alien and citizen, and is larger than the total number of Japanese aliens in both the continental United States and Hawaii combined—but this kind of official confusion about number and status of Japanese resident in the United States was more typical than aberrant. For most practical purposes the government eventually ignored the legal difference between citizen and alien.

At the other end of Pennsylvania Avenue there was also concern about resident Japanese in the months before Pearl Harbor. Franklin Roosevelt, himself a former assistant secretary of the navy, was well aware of the admirals' phobia about Japan and the Japanese, and although, in an article written in the 1920s he had somewhat pooh-poohed the whole "yellow peril—most probable enemy" syndrome, his actions before and after Pearl Harbor demonstrate that even our greatest modern president was not immune to anti-Oriental racism. In the fall of 1941 an amateur, independent White House intelligence apparatus* considered the whole problem of possible sabotage on the West Coast by Japanese Americans.

The report by journalist C. B. Munson, correctly concluded that "for the most part the [West Coast] Japanese are loyal to the United States or, at worst, hope that by remaining quiet they can avoid concentration camps or irresponsible mobs. We do not believe that they would be at least any more disloyal than any other racial group with whom we went to war." Despite this, Munson was convinced that "there are still Japanese in the United States who will tie dynamite around their waist and make a human bomb out of themselves." He was "horrified" to observe that "dams, bridges, power stations, etc., are wholly unguarded everywhere. The harbor of San Pedro could be razed by fire completely by four men with hand grenades and a little study in one night. Dams could be blown and half of lower California might actually die of thirst. . . . One railway bridge at the exit from the mountains in some cases could tie up three or four main railroads."

This report, or at least a one-page summary of it, was read by President Roosevelt. He thought it important enough to send to Secretary of War Henry L. Stimson, just a month before Pearl Harbor, with the instruction that "the guarding of key points should be looked into."[6] Given FDR's partial endorsement, the report is indicative of a propensity to believe that almost anything could be accomplished by fanatical, implacable Orientals. The notion that a major transportation complex could be destroyed by "four men with hand grenades" is so palpably ridiculous that it should have caused the whole report to be rejected out of hand. Yet, it claimed attention at the very highest levels of the American government. Only if we understand that the racist image of the Oriental in the American mind was so strong that many otherwise sensible people could literally believe *anything* about him will we begin to understand why Americans reacted to the Japanese as they did.

A Policy of Restraint

Yet, when war came, on December 7, 1941, no overall internal security plan existed. The FBI, in conjunction with military and naval intelligence, had maintained lists of dangerous Japanese. According to Munson, each of the three West Coast Naval Districts (headquartered in Seattle, San Francisco and Los Angeles) had lists of 250 to 300 suspects, although they admitted privately that perhaps only 40 to 50 on each list were a real "threat." The

*This was a very different kind of operation than that of the so-called White House "plumbers" of the Nixon administration. Its operatives were mainly journalists who offered on-the-spot observations. Yet, it is instructive to note, both stemmed from the tendency of politicians not to trust the professional military intelligence reports. The man who ran this operation, John Franklin Carter, who as a pro-New Deal journalist wrote under the pseudonyms of "Jay Franklin" and "Unofficial Observer," later claimed that his operation was the seed from which the CIA grew. See his correspondence with Allen Dulles in the John Franklin Carter Mss., University of Wyoming.

FBI list was somewhat larger. In any event, internal security forces quickly picked up some 1,500 alien Japanese; when Germany and Italy declared war, some of their nationals were similarly seized (see Document 1). Altogether, the Department of Justice incarcerated some 16,000 enemy aliens, not counting diplomatic and consular personnel. About two-thirds of these were released, paroled, or, in a few cases repatriated. *(Alternative 2: Mass Incarceration of Aliens or Individual Arrests.)*

The relative restraint of this program was due to the fact that the Attorney General, Francis Biddle, as he puts it in his memoirs, "was determined to avoid mass internment, and the persecution of aliens that had characterized the First World War." He also says that Franklin Roosevelt was willing to have all 600,000 German nationals in the United States interned. "I don't care so much about the Italians," Biddle reports the president saying in his offhand manner, "they are a lot of opera singers, but the Germans are different, they may be dangerous."[7] Happily, Biddle did not take this as a directive, and continued to operate with restraint.

Even this policy of restraint resulted in the imprisonment of many individuals who were in no conceivable way a threat to the United States. Although the FBI lists and other documents relating to custody and internment of enemy aliens are still "classified" and thus unavailable to scholars, internal security procedures can be reconstructed. It is clear that the federal government knew little about the Japanese American community. No investigative official of the Department of Justice could either read or write Japanese. The department did have some informants, many of them overzealous, among the American-born Japanese population, but most of its arrests were based on guilt by association. The basic investigative tools seem to have been directories of Japanese American organizations. Most of these organizations had ties, often financial, with the Japanese government. Others were clearly supportive of Japanese imperialism in East Asia. Still others, like Japanese American chambers of commerce, were trade oriented. What the federal government did was simply to take into custody most of the officers and leading lights of those organizations. These included religious organizations, and resulted, in one instance, in a middle-of-the-night arrest of an octogenarian Buddhist priest. Yet, all things considered, the initial performance of American internal security officers, if somewhat overzealous, was relatively restrained. In Britain, for example, after the fall of France in 1940, all German and Austrian aliens—the majority of whom were Jewish refugees from fascism—were interned.

But even liberal Attorney General Biddle was, almost unconsciously, more prone to violate the rights of nonwhite "enemies" than of white "enemies." Understandably the Canadian and Mexican borders were closed to alien enemies immediately following the declarations of war. But in the case of Japanese, the Attorney General's order specified that "all persons of Japanese ancestry, whether citizen or alien" were to be denied either ingress or exit from the United States. Even more serious were the restraints imposed by the Treasury Department on the bank accounts of all enemy aliens. Since Japanese were "aliens ineligible to citizenship" and could not be naturalized, this meant that most adult Japanese residents in the United States could not even get access to their own money. In the week after Pearl Harbor, partially in response to telegrams from Eleanor Roosevelt, who happened to be on the West Coast, Secretary Morgenthau modified the "freeze" order so that Japanese Americans could get a maximum of $100 a month from their bank accounts if they had no other sources of income.[8]

The impact of these early federal actions on the Japanese American community were of enormous importance, both from their very real effect and, perhaps even more significantly, from their psychological impact. The 1,500 men who were interned, for example, although they amounted to a little over one percent of the Japanese American population, represented more than five percent of the adult males in the community. In addition, the interned men were almost always community leaders, so that their sudden departure created an impact far greater than their mere numerical incidence would indicate. Even before war broke out, many young Nisei had come to dread the future. As one of them had written four years earlier, in case of war between the United States and Japan "our properties would be confiscated and most likely (we would be) herded into prison camps—perhaps we would be slaughtered on the spot."[9] Others, who joined the hypernationalistic Japanese American Citizens League, which barred aliens from membership, put their faith in an idealized America: their official creed, written in 1940, insisted that:

> Although some individuals may discriminate against me, I shall never become bitter or lose faith, for I know that such persons are not representative of the majority of the American people.[10]

This almost reflexive patriotism, not untypical for insecure second generation Americans of almost any origin, would be severely tested during the war. What the Japanese American community did not know was that, almost from the initiation of hostilities, there were those in the highest governmental circles who contemplated mass incarceration. The earliest clear evidence of this is found in the "Diary" of Henry Morgenthau, Jr., Roosevelt's secretary of the treasury. In a meeting in Washington, D.C., on December 11, 1941, the treasury secretary and some of his aides debated measures to be taken in regard to the frozen funds of Japanese Americans. In referring to an interdepartmental meeting held the previous day (of which there seems to be no record) Morgenthau argued for more lenient treatment.

> Morgenthau: And then I suddenly woke up in the middle of the night and found myself in bed with [Under Secretary of the Navy James V.] Forrestal and J. Edgar Hoover.
>
> Foley: [Edward Foley, General Counsel, Treasury Department] No time to be thinking about civil liberties when the country is in danger.
>
> Morgenthau: Listen, no-one except Harold Ickes and myself could want to go further [for waging all-out war] . . . so my record speaks for itself. But when it comes to suddenly mopping up a hundred and fifty thousand Japanese and putting them behind barbed wire, irrespective of their status, and consider doing the same with the Germans, I wanted some time to catch my breath. I am sure you are

on my side. Anybody that wants to hurt this country or injure us, put him where he can't do it, but irrespective, indiscriminately, no. . . . [11]

The Growth of Hostility

Although they could not know of this and other secret discussions of their fate, the open and implacable hostility of the California press and radio were immediately apparent. On December 8, 1941, in the same issue that announced the coming of war, the Los Angeles *Times*, the leading newspaper in southern California, editorialized about the menace of the Japanese Americans. California, said the *Times*, was "a zone of danger." It predicted peril from "spies, saboteurs and fifth columnists" and asked the public to be "alert" and "keen-eyed."

> We have thousands of Japanese here. . . . Some, perhaps, many, are . . . good Americans. What the rest may be we do not know, nor can we take a chance in the light of yesterday's demonstration that treachery and double-dealing are major Japanese weapons.

The next day a nationally syndicated rightwing columnist, Westbrook Pegler, proposed that for every hostage murdered by our enemies the United States should strike back by killing "100 victims selected out of [our] concentration camps" which Pegler assumed would be set up for subversive Germans and Italians and "alien Japanese." It should be noted that, for white aliens, the criterion was subversive activity; for nonwhites, mere nationality. Similar examples of hostility to Japanese Americans filled the West Coast media. Even more serious were stories, headlines and broadcasts which created the utterly false impression that Japanese spies, saboteurs and even paramilitary and military groups were everywhere. None of these stories had any basis in fact: amazingly, there was not one demonstrable case of sabotage or espionage committed in the continental United States by a Japanese American during the entire war. But what people believe is often even more important than the facts, and there is overwhelming evidence for the conclusion that the vast majority of white Americans on the Pacific Coast (and not a few Japanese Americans!) came to feel that as long as Japanese Americans remained at large, they could, in Morgenthau's words, "hurt this country." Here are some representative headlines, all taken from the Los Angeles *Times*, a relatively responsible paper:

JAP BOAT FLASHES MESSAGE ASHORE
ENEMY PLANES SIGHTED OVER CALIFORNIA COAST
TWO JAPANESE WITH MAPS AND ALIEN LITERATURE SEIZED
JAP AND CAMERA HELD IN BAY CITY
VEGETABLES FOUND FREE OF POISON
CAPS ON JAPANESE TOMATO PLANTS POINT TO AIR BASE
JAPANESE HERE SENT VITAL DATA TO TOKYO
CHINESE ABLE TO SPOT JAP
MAP REVEALS JAP MENACE
Network of Alien Farms Covers
Strategic Defense Areas over Southland
JAPS PLAN COAST ATTACK IN APRIL WARNS CHIEF
OF KOREAN SPY BAND

It is now clear that a major source for these persistent and mendacious stories were American military officers, especially those connected with the Western Defense Command with headquarters in San Francisco's Presidio. Although, as we have seen, some civilians in Washington had tentatively discussed mass incarceration, the first concrete proposals aimed at the West Coast Japanese emanated from the Presidio. The man in charge was John L. De Witt, a sixty-one year old lieutenant general at the time of Pearl Harbor. It was De Witt and his headquarters staff which exacerbated and stimulated the latent fears of the West Coast population about the yellow peril that had been a nightmare for decades. As the course of the Pacific War produced disaster after disaster during that bleak winter of 1941-42, the growth of such fears was not surprising.

Notes

1. Harold M. Hyman, *To Try Men's Souls* (Berkeley and Los Angeles: University of California Press, 1959), p. 329.

2. Roger Daniels, *Concentration Camps, U.S.A.: Japanese Americans and World War II* (New York: Holt, Rinehart and Winston, 1972). For the anti-Japanese movement through 1924, see Daniels, *The Politics of Prejudice* (Berkeley and Los Angeles: University of California Press, 1962).

3. *Proceedings*, Federal-State Conference on Law Enforcement Problems of National Defense (Washington, D.C., 1940), as cited in Hyman, *To Try Men's Souls*, p. 328.

4. Memorandum, Gullion to Assistant Chief of Staff (G-1), "Internment of Enemy Aliens," August 12, 1940, Record Group 407, National Archives, Washington, D.C.

5. Dingell to FDR, August 18, 1941, Franklin D. Roosevelt Library, Official File 1971, Hyde Park, New York.

6. Munson's report, plus a one-page summary by John Franklin Carter, is attached to a memorandum, FDR to Stimson, November 8, 1941, Franklin D. Roosevelt Library, "Stimson Folder," Hyde Park, New York.

7. Francis Biddle, *In Brief Authority* (New York: Doubleday, 1962), p. 207.

8. For details of this and other early actions see Daniels, *Concentration Camps, U.S.A.* pp. 34-35.

9. *Campanile Review*, Berkeley, California, Fall, 1937.

10. The entire creed may be found in the *Congressional Record*, May 9, 1941, p. A2205.

11. Diary of Henry Morgenthau, Jr., vol. 470, p. 164, Franklin D. Roosevelt Library, Hyde Park, New York. Earlier in the same meeting Morgenthau spoke of people in Los Angeles as "so hysterical they wanted the Army to go out and work the truck farms while they put the Japanese into a concentration camp.", p. 141.

2

"Stern Military Necessity"

General John L. De Witt was a cautious, indecisive officer whom the army would relieve and then retire before the war's end. Even before Pearl Harbor, there is clear evidence of his blatant racism; although it was army policy to accept Asian Americans for general service and blacks for service in segregated units, De Witt wanted neither in his command. When he learned, just after Pearl Harbor, that some of the replacements he had clamored for were going to be Negro, he risked a reprimand by protesting through channels that:

> ... you're filling too many colored groups up on the West Coast. ... there will be a great deal of public reaction out here due to the Jap situation. They feel they've got enough black skinned people around them as it is. Filipinos and Japanese ... I'd rather have a white regiment.[1]

It is possible to reconstruct the atmosphere that existed within De Witt's headquarters from two unique primary sources; the diary of Joseph W. Stilwell and the recordings of telephone conversations between De Witt and his staff and Army GHQ in Washington.*

In December, 1941, Stilwell was a major general and De Witt's chief subordinate in charge of Southern California. As the famed "Vinegar Joe" of the heartbreaking Burma campaigns, Stilwell became legendary for his frankness and biting tongue. Later in the war, for example, he continually referred to Chiang Kai-Shek, China's chief of state, as "the peanut." His diary for December, 1941, kept in pencil in a dime store pocket-sized notebook, recounts in caustic terms the foolish false alarms that emanated from De Witt's headquarters. On December 7, he was informed that a Japanese air raid was taking place in San Francisco. When this proved to be false, Stilwell noted that his superior was "kind of jittery." Two days later he was told that thirty-four Japanese ships were between San Francisco and Los Angeles, and, on December 11, a phone call alerted him to the presence of the main Japanese fleet 164 miles off San Francisco. When this too, proved false, Stilwell noted that "I believed it, like a damn fool." Two days later Stilwell refused to believe still another false alarm, warning of an "imminent" attack on Los Angeles. By this time Stilwell had lost all patience with his commander, whom he described as a "jackass,"

---

*In that pre-electronic age, the conversations were actually recorded on records and later transcribed. All parties to the conversations seemed to be aware that recording was going on.

14

noting that the Presidio staff was "amateur." He also inscribed a maxim in his diary: "Rule: the higher the headquarters, the more important is calm." [2]

De Witt's headquarters was anything but calm. He and his staff exuded an infectious panic that was, if anything, reflected and magnified by the rather paranoid style endemic to the American West Coast. It was from this amateurish, panic-ridden headquarters that the first *military* proposal for mass evacuation was developed less than seventy-two hours after the attack on Pearl Harbor. On the evening of December 10, De Witt's staff became convinced that twenty thousand Japanese in the San Francisco Bay Area were about to participate in an armed uprising, possibly coordinated with an invasion. A hasty scheme to preempt this alleged revolt by taking all these people into military custody actually received tentative approval by the area commander, a General Benedict. This harebrained scheme was, happily, aborted on the advice of the local head of the Federal Bureau of Investigation, Nat Pieper, who informed the army that their "reliable source" was a former employee of his whom he had fired because of similar "wild imaginings." The notion of an armed revolt by the peaceful Japanese American population was ridiculous: the figure of twenty thousand armed men slightly exceeded the total number of Japanese men, women and children in the region. Nevertheless De Witt's headquarters passed the whole fantasy on to Washington and recommended that "plans be made for large-scale internment." (See Document 2). Nine days later, on December 19, 1941, General De Witt officially recommended that "action be initiated at the earliest practicable date to collect all alien subjects fourteen years of age and over, of enemy nations and remove them" to the interior of the United States and hold them "under restraint after removal" so they could not come back. This proposal would have involved not only incarceration of Japanese, but of German and Italian aliens as well. The age limit of fourteen apparently came from the federal statutes on wartime internment, but those statutes referred specifically to males only. No provision whatever was made for the minor children of such enemy aliens, many of whom, of course, would be American citizens.[3]

This proposal was never acted upon. It would have been an undertaking of enormous magnitude and would have had serious political repercussions. There were, in the United States, more than a million European enemy aliens: about seven hundred thousand Italians and more than three hundred thousand Germans. More than fifty thousand Italian aliens lived in California, most of them in and around San Francisco. As we shall see, any proposals to incarcerate *them*, quickly and properly drew protests from many sectors of the larger community. The nonwhite Japanese, however, had fewer defenders. The proposal, however, was important. We have already noted that some kind of mass round-up of Japanese aliens had been discussed at the highest levels in Washington early in the month. De Witt's proposal, once it was inserted into the army's bureaucratic and authoritarian machine, soon found its supporters.

The Support of Military Opinions

The most crucial of these supporters was an obscure but important army bureaucrat, Major General Allen W. Gullion who was the army's Provost Marshal General (PMG), and, as such, its chief law enforcement officer. He had been the army's Judge Advocate General, which is the highest legal office within the military establishment. In both of these jobs he had been increasingly concerned with the problems of exercising military control over civilians in wartime. Since the fall of France, in June, 1940, the army—and the general public—had become convinced, erroneously, that traitorous civilians, called "fifth columnists," had played a major role in the French collapse. By August, 1940, Army G-2 (Intelligence) officially took the position that a similar phenomenon might occur in the United States and that, in case of war, "the Military would certainly have to provide for the arrest and temporary holding of a large number of suspects." Gullion, as Judge Advocate General, maintained in 1940 that within the United States, as long as the civilian courts were functioning, the military did not have the authority even to participate in the apprehension of civilian citizens.[4] If martial law were declared, it would be another matter. Martial law was never declared within the United States (it was in effect throughout the war in the Territory of Hawaii). Had Gullion held to his prewar opinion, the evacuation of the Japanese Americans might never have taken place. But Gullion and the people in G-2 had been hypothesizing about white people; where Asians were concerned, the color of the law itself could change. That change was abetted, unwittingly, by a decision made by Chief of Staff George C. Marshall in early December; just four days after Pearl Harbor the West Coast, plus Alaska, was declared a "Theater of Operations," and General De Witt was given expanded authority. This made him, in the bureaucratic parlance of the War Department, "the man on the ground," and gave to his confused views a weight they would not otherwise have held.

Precisely what De Witt thought at any given moment is sometimes quite difficult to reconstruct because, as we shall see, his opinions vacillated. Eventually, however, his views—or at least a significant part of them—came to prevail as far as the West Coast Japanese were concerned, even though they were opposed by his own direct superiors in the army hierarchy. It is important, therefore, for any analyst of the decision to relocate the Japanese Americans to attempt to understand him.

One salient fact about De Witt was that he was an old man; although he and Chief of Staff Marshall had both been born in 1880, the latter was a vigorous sixty-one with his most important work before him. De Witt's career had actually peaked in 1939 with his promotion to lieutenant general. Like Marshall he was not a West Pointer and he was one of the few men in the army to call the Chief of Staff by his first name. Although here we shall be concerned solely with his role in the relocation decision, it is worth noting that his overall administration of the Western Defense Command left much to be desired. In January, 1942, for example, the Chief of Army Field Forces,

Lieutenant General Wesley J. McNair told Stilwell that "De Witt has gone crazy and requires ten refusals before he realizes it is 'No.' "[5] De Witt, who had the example of the disgrace of another contemporary, Lieutenant General Walter C. Short, the army commander in Hawaii at the time of the Japanese attack, was apparently determined that no Pearl Harbor would occur on the West Coast. He had an extreme case of what Marshall used to call "localitis"—the feeling that his own theater was the most important, and constantly called on the War Department for an ever greater commitment of troops to the West Coast. To the planners in Washington, intent above all on creating an offensive army for operations in Europe, all such requests were anathema. As a result, De Witt never got his fourth star and was eventually relieved of his command in September, 1943, and given the then meaningless job of commandant of the Army and Navy Staff College. Yet, for a few crucial weeks in the dark winter of 1941-42, the opinions of this redundant old general, whose views of Asians had probably been shaped by four tours of garrison duty in the Philippines, would be of critical importance to the lives of 110,000 West Coast Japanese Americans and would help shape the decisions made about them by the American government.

It must be understood, however, that De Witt was merely an instrument. Had not his views found resounding support in other sectors of American life—and been reinforced by that support—the evacuation would never have taken place. But the evacuation was not an "inevitable" phenomenon either. Historical decisions, good and bad, are made by men, and De Witt is one of the key men involved here.

By the last week of December, 1941, he and the army Provost Marshal, Allen Gullion, were in direct telephone contact. This was outside of the normal chain of command. De Witt did not inform his superiors of these conversations for some time. Like everyone in the old army, De Witt and Gullion, who were of an age, knew each other, but apparently not well. Gullion, in typically bureaucratic fashion, was trying to expand the limited scope and size of his functions as Provost Marshal. On December 22, 1941, he formally requested the Secretary of War, Henry L. Stimson, to press for the transfer of responsibility for the conduct of the enemy alien program from the Department of Justice to the War Department, from civilian to military jurisdiction. He clearly got some encouragement from the secretary's office, probably from Assistant Secretary of War John J. McCloy, who had been given great latitude in such matters by the aging secretary. (Stimson had been born in 1867; McCloy in 1895.) McCloy was an almost archetypical member of the eastern Republican establishment. A product of private schools, an elite college (*cum laude*, Amherst '16), and Harvard Law School, he had served as a captain in the Field Artillery in World War I. He spent the next two decades in Wall Street law firms, coming to the War Department as an expert consultant to the secretary of war in October, 1940. What first recommended McCloy to Stimson was that as a lawyer handling claims arising out of the "Black Tom" case (a demonstrated instance of German sabotage of an American munitions plant in New Jersey in July, 1916), he had a presumed

expertise about German subversive methods. Within six months he became
assistant secretary, a post he held throughout the war. As Stimson describes
him in his memoirs, "so varied were his labors and so catholic his interests
that they defy summary. For five years McCloy was the man who handled
everything that no one else happened to be handling."[6] Among the things
that no one else was handling was "enemy aliens" so, when the army began
seriously to consider doing something about the Japanese menace on the West
Coast it naturally became the province of the department's countersubversive
expert.

By the end of December the War Department began applying pressure on
the Justice Department for more rigorous control of the West Coast Japanese
and other aliens (see Document 2-a). On December 26, De Witt called Gullion
and told him that he wanted firmer steps taken by the FBI against Japanese
and enemy aliens. At that moment, he was opposed to mass incarceration:

> I thought that thing out to my satisfaction. ... if we go ahead and
> arrest the 93,000 Japanese, native born and foreign born, we are going
> to have an awful job on our hands and we are liable to alienate the loyal
> Japanese from disloyal. ... I'm very doubtful that it would be common
> sense procedure to try and intern or to intern 117,000 Japanese in this
> theater. ... I told the governors of all the states that those people
> should be watched better if they were watched by the police and the
> people of the community in which they live and have been living for
> years ... and then inform the FBI or the military authorities of any
> suspicious action so we could take necessary steps to handle it ...
> rather than try to intern those people, men, women and children, and
> hold them under military control and under guard. I don't think it's a
> sensible thing to do, ... I'd rather go along the way we are now ...
> rather than attempt any such whole-sale internment. ... An American
> citizen, after all, is an American citizen. And while they may not be
> loyal, I think we can weed the disloyal out of the loyal and lock them
> up if necessary.[7]

Moving Away From Restraint

De Witt did not hold these restrained views long; they are directly contrary
to the mass alien round-up he had proposed to the War Department seven
days earlier, and to the position he would later take and maintain. Given the
available evidence, it is impossible to account for his sudden shifts of opinion
by rational analysis. Attorney General Biddle's notion that "he was apt to
waver under popular pressure, a characteristic arising from his tendency to
reflect the views of the last man to whom he talked" may be a valid one.[8]
What is clear is that after his December 26 statement he came more and more
under the influence of Provost Marshal General Gullion, who, at the end of
December, sent the Chief of his Aliens Division, Major Karl R. Bendetsen, on
a flying cross-country visit to De Witt's headquarters. Bendetsen, despite his
low rank, became a key figure in the decision-making process and seemed to
have greater influence over De Witt than members of his own staff. De Witt's
own chief of intelligence, Lieutenant Colonel John R. Weckerling, consistently advised against mass evacuation, and may have helped shape De Witt's

restrained late December views.[9] But, as time passed and the pressures mounted, Gullion and above all Bendetsen, seemed to have the general's ear.

Bendetsen was not a career officer, but a civilian lawyer in uniform. Born in 1907 in Aberdeen, Washington, he was educated at Stanford where he earned an A.B. in 1929 and an LL.B. three years later. He entered the army as a captain in the judge advocate's department in 1940 and quickly rose to colonel by early 1942. Prior to becoming head of the Aliens Division of the newly formed Office of the Provost Marshal General, his military service had been focused on the drafting of legislative proposals and the administering of war plants seized by the army due to labor disputes. In his own words he "conceived method, formulated details and directed evacuation of 120,000 persons of Japanese ancestry from military areas," for which a grateful nation awarded him the Distinguished Service Medal.

After his end-of-year trip to De Witt's headquarters, Bendetsen became a chief army spokesman and planner regarding matters Japanese. A key problem for the men in the Provost Marshal General's office was the continuing responsibility of the Department of Justice for alien enemies, and the department's continuing reluctance to move as far or as fast as the army planners wished. On the day before Christmas, for example, De Witt had wired the Adjutant General requesting that the Attorney General empower the West Coast offices of the FBI to ignore normal due process procedures in searching any house where an alien enemy lived. In response to this, two days later, Gullion told De Witt that: "I've reached the point where I think I'm going to ask the Secretary [of War Stimson] to tell the President the Attorney General is not functioning."[10] On New Year's Day Gullion's deputy, Colonel Archer Lerch told De Witt that "before Bendetsen left here . . . he drafted a proposed amendment to the Executive Order which would place in the hands of the Secretary of War the right to take over aliens when he thought it was necessary." However, Lerch continued, Biddle's aides James Rowe and Edward Ennis had been so apologetic about their department's slowness that he felt that "it wasn't quite fair to process that thing through until they had failed to do it better."[11]

On January 3, Bendetsen, at De Witt's headquarters, spelled out in a memorandum the kinds of authority the men in the office of the Provost Marshal General wanted derogated to themselves. The memorandum was addressed to General De Witt in the hope that if those measures were pressed by a commander in the field they would have more weight.

> It is necessary that the Attorney General delegate to the FBI Special Agents in charge authority to issue alien enemy apprehension warrants.
>
> . . . .
>
> It further requires an immediate and complete registration of all alien enemies. This should provide for photographs and fingerprints and for the maintenence of duplicate sets of such records in the communities in which the registrants reside as well as at a central office. This should form the basis for a "Pass and Permit System" and for a "Continental" travel regulations system.[12]

Bendetsen and others in the PMG's office knew well that the attorney general was opposed to the setting up of a massive internal security bureaucracy. In his conclusion, he explicitly proposed that if the Department of Justice was unwilling to assume this responsibility then the War Department must implement it. As the Chief of the Aliens Division of the PMG's office, Bendetsen would be the logical person to be in charge of this expanded system, and, once in such a job could expect general's stars; his boss, Gullion, could have expected a promotion too.

Notes taken at a conference in General De Witt's office the next day probably show Bendetsen's influence. The West Coast commander had "little confidence that the enemy aliens are law-abiding or loyal in any sense of the word. Some of them, yes; many, no. Particularly the Japanese. I have no confidence in their loyalty whatsoever. I am speaking now of the native born Japanese—117,000—and 42,000 in California alone."[13]

By the end of the first week in January the training branch of the General Staff (G-3) made a policy recommendation (approved by Chief of Staff George C. Marshall two weeks later) that all soldiers of Japanese descent not be given specialized training and after training they be assigned to units in the Zone of the Interior and, in those units, "not be assigned positions in units or installations where they might gain valuable information or be able to execute damage to important installations; nor will they be grouped in specific units." On that same day several military and naval commanders on the West Coast recommended drastic programs aimed at removing large numbers of civilians. In identical language, two admirals commanding adjoining naval districts recommended that "all enemy aliens" be evacuated from West Coast states and "that all American-born of Japanese racial origin who cannot show actual severance of allegiance to the Japanese Government be classified as enemy aliens."[14] Major General Kenyon A. Joyce, commanding general of the Ninth Army Corps headquartered at Ft. Lewis, Washington, associated himself with these naval recommendations. Joyce was told by De Witt on the phone that day, with apparent regret, that "they [not specified, but presumably higher headquarters] won't allow a mass exodus or mass evacuation." Joyce, for his part, was sure that sabotage and "fifth columnists" had played a key role in the disaster at Pearl Harbor and that

> any hostile attack against the Northwestern Sector will be characterized by a similar treacherous activity. From what is known of the Japanese character and mentality it is also considered dangerous to rely on the loyalty of native born persons of Japanese blood unless such loyalty can be affirmatively demonstrated.[15]

Thus, a full month after Pearl Harbor, despite a certain amount of discussion in various official circles, both civilian and military, few concrete measures had been taken specifically against Japanese Americans, although it is apparent that enemy alien Japanese were subject to greater restraints than were alien Germans and Italians, and that native born Japanese Americans were the only second generation group to be singled out for special attention and discrimination. Perhaps even more important, in the final analysis, were things that were not done. In that month, a time of unprecedented national unity, governmental leaders, from the president down to mayors, could have conducted an educational campaign designed to quiet popular fears about the "yellow peril." Instead most officials, by omission or commission, either ignored or exacerbated the problem. At the national level, Fiorello La Guardia, who in December, 1941, was serving in the dual capacity of mayor of New York City and director of the federal Office of Civilian Defense, made two separate post-Pearl Harbor statements about enemy aliens. As the nation's most prominent Italian American politician, he spoke not only for Italians, but for German aliens as well, suggesting quite properly that all such persons be presumed loyal until evidence of individual disloyalty appeared. He pointedly said nothing about Japanese aliens. In 1924 La Guardia had been one of three congressmen who had spoken on the floor of the House in favor of granting an immigration quota to Japan, but after Pearl Harbor Japanese Americans lost even his verbal protection. (Two and a half years later, in April, 1944, La Guardia publicly opposed the resettlement of any Japanese Americans in New York City.)

Demands from Civilians

California officials could not ignore the Japanese in their state. Before Pearl Harbor, the state's liberal Democratic Governor, Culbert L. Olson, had argued that even in case of war with Japan, Japanese Americans should continue to enjoy their personal liberty and other benefits of American citizenship. Although this was an unpopular stand, Olson correctly pointed out that equal protection under the law was a "basic tenet" of American government. The governor's devotion to the spirit of the constitution was apparently destroyed by the Japanese attack. On December 8, he told the press that he was thinking of ordering all Japanese, alien or citizen, to stay in their houses "to avoid riot and disturbance."[16] Olson never issued this order (one suspects that his legalistic attorney general, Earl Warren, told him that it would be illegal without a martial law proclamation), but, as we shall see, he consistently cooperated with federal officials to inhibit the liberty of those Japanese American citizens of California whose rights he had sworn to protect in his oath of office.

At the local level, there was considerably less restraint. Beginning in the first week in January, local West Coast officials and citizens began to bombard federal and state officials of all categories to "do something" about "all the Japs who were running loose" on the West Coast.[17] This pressure, probably stimulated by the press and radio, and not subject to any significant restraint by responsible officials, began to have its effect on West Coast congressmen. In December, these congressmen had made no public outcry for mass incarceration or evacuation. In fact, when a demand for drastic treatment of resident Japanese was made on December 15 by the House's leading racist demagogue, Mississippi Democrat John Rankin, he was rebutted by California Republican Leland Ford.

"These people are American-born," Ford insisted. "They cannot be deported . . . whether we like it or whether we do not. This is their country. . . . [When] they join the armed forces . . . they must take the oath of allegiance . . . and I see no particular reason at this particular time why they should not. I believe that every one of these people should make a clear, clean acknowledgement [of loyalty]."[18]

By the first week of January, however, Ford was forwarding to Secretary of War Stimson demands that he had received from his constituents calling for mass evacuation of Japanese from vital areas. By January 16 Ford had become an exponent of mass evacuation himself. On that day he wrote Stimson, telling him of the "many" communications on the subject he had received and formally proposing that, "to prevent any fifth column activity":

That all Japanese, whether citizens or not, be placed in inland concentration camps. As justification for this, I submit that if an American born Japanese, who is a citizen, is really patriotic and wishes to make his contribution to the safety and welfare of this country, right here is his opportunity to do so, namely, that by permitting himself to be placed in a concentration camp, he would be making his sacrifice, and he should be willing to do it if he is patriotic and working for us. As against his sacrifice, millions of other native born citizens are willing to lay down their lives, which is a far greater sacrifice, of course, than being placed in a concentration camp. Therefore any loyal Japanese should not hesitate to do that which is absolutely the best for the country, and to operate in such a manner that his particular activity would be for the greatest benefit.[19]

The chop-logic of this proposal almost defies analysis, but it is typical of the classic "Catch 22," "heads I win, tails you lose" situation in which Japanese Americans were placed in the weeks after Pearl Harbor. That most, but not all, of their community leaders eventually decided to "go along" with the evacuation proposals is hardly surprising. Ford's letter closed with a request for Stimson's opinion on the matter. Ten days later, on January 26, 1942, the war secretary replied in a letter that had been drafted by Bendetsen, the War Department's new resident expert on the Japanese, who was now back from the West Coast. The letter is worth reading in full, for it is one of the first documents to show how far thinking at the highest official levels had progressed with regard to mass evacuation.

Dear Mr. Ford:

This will acknowledge receipt of your letter of January 16, 1942, proposing the evacuation of all Japanese from the Pacific Coast and their internment inland in order to prevent fifth-column activity.

The internment of over a hundred thousand people, and their evacuation inland, presents a very real problem. While the necessity for firm measures to insure the maximum war effort cannot be questioned, the proposal suggested by you involves many complex considerations.

Responsibility and authority for the determination of the necessity for internment in continental United States has been delegated by the President to the Attorney General by proclamations dated December 7 and 8, 1941. Those ordered interned by the Department of Justice are turned over to the Army for custody. The Army is prepared to provide internment facilities in the interior to the extent necessary.

The Army is submitting recommendations to the Attorney General for designation by him of restricted areas on the Pacific Coast. This, together with the pending alien registration directed by the President, should formulate the basis for a definite program of security from fifth-column activity emanating from this source. I take the liberty of suggesting that you present your views to the Attorney General for consideration.

I am grateful for your interest.

Sincerely yours,
Henry L. Stimson
Secretary of War[20]

Stimson's letter can only have encouraged Congressman Ford and his West Coast colleagues. Without ever complaining directly, Stimson suggested that the Department of Justice, headed by a New Dealer, was governing the action that the army could take. In addition, the letter deliberately evaded the whole question of citizenship. By talking about "internment," a process applicable only to aliens, and by citing authority contained in presidential proclamations which referred only to enemy aliens, Stimson's letter deliberately blurred the distinction between citizen and alien, at least as far as Japanese Americans were concerned. It is quite possible, of course, that the busy war secretary did not subject Bendetsen's draft to rigorous analysis before signing it, but even if this was the case it in no way diminishes his responsibility. The letter, of course, accurately represented the position of the provost marshal general's office.

False Fears and Wrong Information

While an answer to Congressman Ford's letter was being drafted, General De Witt forwarded to Washington his first concrete proposals for the evacuation. Although he had originally promised them by January 9, his not very efficient headquarters was only able to submit them on January 21. These first recommendations were relatively modest. They called for setting up in California eighty-six "category A" zones, from which all enemy aliens were to be barred, and eight "category B" zones, in which all enemy aliens were to be closely controlled under a "pass and permit" system. Many of the "category A" zones were desolate stretches of coast; their total enemy alien population was less than seven thousand. About fifty thousand enemy aliens in the "category B" areas would have been affected, but more than half of these were Italians and only about a third were Japanese. Two weeks later, on February 3, De Witt's headquarters sent on similar plans for creating "A" and "B" areas in Washington, Oregon and Arizona.

War Secretary Stimson approved De Witt's proposals of January 21, and four days later recommended formally to the attorney general that they be put into effect. His recommendation to Biddle included false information, supplied by De Witt, about fifth column activity on the West Coast.

In recent conferences with General De Witt, he has expressed great apprehension because of the presence on the Pacific Coast of many thousand alien enemies. As late as yesterday, 24 January, he stated over the telephone that shore-to-ship and ship-to-shore radio communications, undoubtedly coordinated by intelligent enemy control were continually operating. A few days ago it was reported by military observers on the Pacific coast that not a single ship had sailed from our Pacific ports without being subsequently attacked. General De Witt's apprehensions have been confirmed by recent visits of military observers from the War Department to the Pacific coast.

The alarming and dangerous situation just described, in my opinion, calls for immediate and stringent action. [21]

This letter, like the one to Congressman Ford, had been drafted by the PMG's office. The "military observers" seem to have been the lawyer in uniform, Karl Bendetsen. We now know that there was little Japanese naval activity off the California coast. The Japanese high command did assign nine modern submarines to operate there, but the activities of these vessels were amazingly ineffective. Only four of the nine engaged in attacks on surface vessels, sinking two tankers and one freighter in December. There had been a plan for these undersea craft to surface and engage in simultaneous shelling of coastal cities on Christmas Eve, but this plan was abandoned by the Japanese high command in late December and the submarines were recalled. At the time of Stimson's letter, there had been no Japanese forces off California for more than a month. In February, two Japanese submarines, the I-8 and the I-17, returned to West Coast waters. The first patrolled from San Francisco north to Washington "without encountering any enemy vessels" and returned to Japan. The second sub, apparently under more competent command (it had sunk one of the four tankers in December), was the only Japanese naval vessel during the entire war to attack the continental United States. It surfaced north of Santa Barbara on the evening of February 23, just as a Roosevelt fireside chat was going on the air, and lobbed thirteen 5½-inch shells at some oil storage tanks on an otherwise desolate hillside. No hits on the tanks were scored, and the I-17 returned home.

The next night there occurred what is usually called the "Battle of Los Angeles." After a night of jittery alarm antiaircraft batteries began to fire about 3:00 A.M. Other batteries, hearing the firing, opened up, and, by dawn, some 1,400 three-inch antiaircraft shells had been exploded in the air over Los Angeles. They shot nothing down—there was nothing up there to hit—but as the shell fragments fell to the ground they damaged dozens of automobiles. The navy officially concluded that the army had no excuse for opening fire but the army insisted that there were "unidentified aircraft" in the area.

De Witt's reports to Stimson via the PMG's office greatly magnified Japanese military activity, and it is difficult to believe that such magnification, after the first few days of panic, was not deliberate. As the official army history puts it, by the end of December "De Witt himself recognized that there was no longer any immediate danger of an invasion in force." [22] He did not, however, share this estimate of the situation with the public which was led to believe that the danger of invasion was a real possibility.

As for the radio messages that De Witt and his subordinates kept reporting, they simply did not exist. No official military document contains a report of such activity; there were no such broadcasts monitored by the Federal Communications Commission, which was looking for them. Nor were there any instances whatsoever of sabotage on the West Coast. Yet, some members of De Witt's intelligence staff were convinced that there was an "espionage net containing Japanese aliens, first and second generation Japanese [and others] ... thoroughly organized and working underground." By January 24, Lieutenant General De Witt had concocted a theory which reconciled his preconceptions about a Japanese American fifth column and the embarrassing fact that these fifth columnists hadn't done anything. "We know there are radios along the coast and we know they are communicating at sea," he told Bendetsen on the telephone January 24. "They may be communicating with each other, but the fact that nothing has happened so far is well let me say more or less ominous, in that I feel that in view of the fact that we have had no sporadic attempts at sabotage that there is control being exercised. . . ."[23]

Like Congressman Ford, General De Witt was playing "Catch 22" with the Japanese Americans. If there had been sabotage, he would have used that as an excuse for recommending mass evacuation. Since there had been no sabotage, that too could form a basis for recommending mass evacuation! Heads I win, tails you lose. This is not to say that General De Witt was not sincere. His natural caution plus his racist preconceptions about the wily Oriental combined to produce this paranoid reaction. The climate of opinion on the West Coast of the United States in early 1942 was such that De Witt was able to convince otherwise rational civilian leaders that what Stilwell had called his "amateur imaginings" were sound military thinking. Perhaps the most impressive of his converts was Earl Warren, then attorney general of California and later the greatest chief justice of this century. Warren, who had met privately with De Witt, put the general's thesis more eloquently in a public congressional hearing held in San Francisco on February 21, 1942:

Unfortunately [many] are of the opinion that because we have had no sabotage and no fifth column activities in this State . . . that none have been planned for us. But I take the view that this is the most ominous sign in our whole situation. It convinces me more than perhaps any other factor that the sabotage we are to get, the fifth column activities we are to get, are timed just like Pearl Harbor was timed and just like the invasion of France, and of Denmark, and of Norway, and all of those other countries.

I believe that we are just being lulled into a false sense of security and that the only reason we haven't had disaster in California is because it has been timed for a different date. . . . Our day of reckoning is bound to come in that regard.[24]

This local feeling of living under some kind of invisible deadline for mass sabotage and unnamed horrors was heightened on January 25 with the publication of the so-called Roberts Report on the disaster at Pearl Harbor. A Republican Supreme Court Justice, Owen J. Roberts, had accepted the responsibility from Roosevelt for making a preliminary report on the causes of our unpreparedness in Hawaii. One of the justice's conclusions was that the operations of "Japanese spies and saboteurs," some of whom had "no open relations with the Japanese foreign service" had greatly increased the effectiveness of the attack.[25] Although we now know that this was not true—Justice Roberts was apparently deceived by oral statements of military and naval officers—it was what people had expected and was almost universally accepted as true. Roberts also was highly critical of prewar counterespionage activity in Hawaii and implied that the FBI had been made ineffective by being held too closely to the letter of the Constitution. A major conclusion that could be and was drawn from Justice Roberts's report was that sterner measures in Hawaii could have prevented and lessened the disaster and that something should be done to prevent a similar occurrence on the West Coast.

Military Pressures for Evacuation: California and Hawaii

Given this climate of opinion, it is not surprising that Attorney General Biddle and the Justice Department acceded rather quickly to the De Witt-Stimson request for exclusion of enemy aliens from the supposedly sensitive "A" and "B" areas in California. It issued a formal statement announcing its decision on January 29, and quite reasonably gave aliens in the affected areas almost a month, until February 24, to make their departure (see Document 4). In agreeing to do this the Justice Department rationalized that it sacrificed no principle, since only enemy aliens were directly affected. But once Biddle and his aides began to issue orders whose only basis was the desire of military officials, they had begun to abdicate their responsibility for internal security.

In addition, the Justice Department, to show its willingness to cooperate, established a liaison between itself and De Witt's headquarters, the Western Defense Command, by naming a department official, Thomas C. Clark, as Co-Ordinator of the Alien Enemy Program on the West Coast, and dispatching him to California. Clark, who later became Attorney General under Truman, and who was eventually appointed by Truman to the Supreme Court, was forty-one years old and had been in the Justice Department for four years. Since 1940 he had been in charge of the department's Antitrust Division on the West Coast and thus knew something of the local situation and local politicians. In his memoirs Biddle characterized his appointment of Clark as "not a fortunate one." According to the Attorney General, Clark was a "wary but amiable Texan with a predilection to please those with whom he was immediately associated."[26] Clark quickly became an advocate for some kind of mass relocation—contrary to the wishes of his superiors in the department—and won accolades from General De Witt and others for his cooperative attitude. About a week after he had been on the job, for example, California Attorney General Earl Warren told the California Joint Immigration Committee—a long established and influential nativist group with which he had been associated—that they should work for mass evacuation through Clark "who is in direct contact with Biddle all the time. . . . You will find him a very approachable fellow."[27]

While the Department of Justice was giving in to Stimson, the top brass of the army, for the first time, began to consider the problem of the West Coast Japanese. Although there may have been unrecorded discussions, the surviving records do not indicate that Chief of Staff George C. Marshall and his direct associates had in any way considered the situation prior to the end of January, 1942. A memorandum dated January 26 written by one of Marshall's deputies, Brigadier General Mark W. Clark (no relation to the Clark in Justice), indicates that the General Staff became aware of De Witt's proposals only on January 24. Noting that the secretary of war had sent the West Coast commander's recommendations to the attorney general who had "full authority to take the action," the memorandum recommended that nothing be done unless the attorney general refused to act. Chief of Staff Marshall annotated this memorandum "hold for me until Feb. 1" (see Document 4).

On January 30, 1942, concern about Japanese in Hawaii was raised in a cabinet meeting, with Secretary of the Navy Frank Knox and President Roosevelt himself expressing alarm. Stimson explained to Marshall his concern over "what steps are being taken or planned for the removal of dangerous Japanese from Hawaii" and reported to Marshall that Justice Roberts and his board considered the situation in the islands as most serious.[28] The problem of Japanese in Hawaii was a vexing one for the military and it is both useful and instructive to compare the situation in the islands with that on the West Coast and to note the quite different treatment meted out in each. There were in Hawaii, according to the census of 1940, more than 150,000 persons of Japanese ancestry and they amounted to more than 37 percent of the population. Almost 80 percent of them, 120,000 people, were native born and thus citizens (see Document 5). *(Alternative 3: Mass Incarceration of Hawaiian Japanese, Alien and Citizen.)*

Two weeks after the Japanese attack the army commander in Hawaii, Lieutenant Delos C. Emmons whom Marshall had handpicked to replace the disgraced General Short, reported to the War Department that careful investigation had disclosed that there had been no sabotage during or after the Pearl Harbor attack and that, with the exception of one Nisei on the tiny island of Niihau who collaborated briefly with a downed Japanese pilot and then committed suicide, no act of hostility against the United States had been committed by a resident Japanese of either generation. General Emmons publicly pledged that the Japanese population in Hawaii would be accorded fair treatment if the inhabitants continued to demonstrate their loyalty.

It should not be inferred from this that Emmons and other commanders responsible for Hawaii were civil libertarians. Emmons himself had little faith in the loyalty of the Japanese population if a Japanese invasion should occur. But the Japanese were vital to the continued functioning of the Hawaiian economy, for which they provided much of the skilled labor. The evacuation or incarceration of more than a third of the population would have created serious manpower problems.

But the politicians in Washington did not see it that way. As early as December 19, Roosevelt's cabinet decided that all Japanese aliens in Hawaii should be interned by the army on one of the smaller islands. Emmons successfully resisted this move, arguing as the "man on the ground" that it was impracticable. When informed of the second cabinet discussion of the Hawaiian Japanese on January 30, Emmons agreed that total evacuation to the mainland would be desirable. This, of course, would require a great deal of shipping that was simply not available. On February 9 he received a War Department order directing him to get rid of all Japanese civilians employed by the army. Emmons protested that there were no possible replacements for these needed workers, and argued that although "the Japanese question" was both "delicate and dangerous" it "should be handled by those in direct contact with the situation." The War Department cancelled its order.

The sparring between Hawaii and Washington continued for months, but Emmons won all the rounds. On February 27, *after* the decision to evacuate the West Coast Japanese had been made, the subject of the Hawaiian Japanese came up in the cabinet for a third time. According to Secretary Stimson's notes of the meeting, Navy Secretary Knox again brought up and urged vigorously the "removal of Japs from Oahu" and suggested placing them all on the island of Molokai, better known as a leper colony.[29] Stimson, having been briefed by Marshall, pointed out some of the difficulties and the matter was left unsettled. Again in March and April, chiefly at the instigation of Knox but with the support of President Roosevelt, proposals for some kind of mass evacuation in the Hawaiian Islands were made. The army continued to resist, on grounds of expediency. Finally, in mid-July, a highly unusual memorandum, signed by both Marshall as army Chief of Staff and Admiral Ernest J. King, Commander in Chief of the fleet, was sent to the president, arguing that mass evacuation was "not feasible," although it did request authorization to ship as many as fifteen thousand persons from Hawaii to the mainland (see Document 5). Faced with a joint recommendation from his chief military officials, President Roosevelt indicated his approval. In fact, only a fraction of these were removed. Altogether, 1,875 Hawaiian residents of Japanese ancestry—the overwhelming majority of them American citizens—were shipped to the relocation centers which had been established in the interior of the United States. Navy Secretary Knox and some members of Roosevelt's entourage sporadically raised the question of further evacuation of Hawaiian Japanese but, after mid-July, 1942, it seems not to have been seriously reconsidered.

Thus, we see the differential treatment accorded to Japanese Americans in Hawaii and California. The islands had been the initial theater of war and certainly would have been subject to serious attack before the West Coast. The concentration of Japanese was much higher there, and, by any kind of rational analysis if Japanese Americans were a danger anywhere, it was in Hawaii. But in Hawaii, real military judgment prevailed. Hawaii was under martial law. It was still a territory, so its residents were not able to participate meaningfully in the American political process. In California and elsewhere on the Pacific Coast, as we shall see, it was political as well as military pressure that brought about the evacuation, although the justifications for it were always couched in terms of "stern military necessity."

Notes

1. Telephone conversation, De Witt and General Green, January 31, 1942, Office of Chief of Staff, Binder #2, from Stetson Conn, "Notes" (personal files).

2. Theodore H. White, ed., *The Stilwell Papers* (New York: W. Sloane Associates, 1948), pp. 2-11.

3. Stetson Conn, "Japanese Evacuation from the West Coast," Stetson Conn, Rose C. Engleman, and Byron Fairchild, *United States Army in World War II: The Western Hemisphere: Guarding the United States and Its Outposts,* (Washington, D.C.: U.S. Government Printing Office, 1964), pp. 116-18.

4. Memorandum, Gullion to Assistant Chief of Staff (G-1), "Internment of Enemy Aliens," August 12, 1940, Record Group 407, National Archives, Washington, D.C.

5. White, *Stilwell Papers*, p. 23.

6. Henry L. Stimson and McGeorge Bundy, *On Active Service in Peace and War* (New York: Harper, 1948), p. 342.

7. Telephone conversation, De Witt and Gullion, December 26, 1941, Stetson Conn, "Notes."

8. Francis Biddle, *In Brief Authority* (New York: Doubleday, 1962), p. 215.

9. Interview with General John R. Weckerling, U.S.A. (ret.), Orlando, Florida, November, 1972.

10. Telephone conversation, De Witt and Gullion, December 26, 1941, Stetson Conn, "Notes."

11. Telephone conversation, De Witt and Lerch, January 1, 1942, Stetson Conn, "Notes."

12. Memorandum, Bendetsen to De Witt, January 3, 1942, Record Group 394, National Archives, Washington, D.C.

13. Notes on January 4, 1942, conference, Stetson Conn, "Notes."

14. Stetson Conn, "Japanese Evacuation from the West Coast," p. 119.

15. Telephone conversation, De Witt and Joyce, January 8, 1942, Record Group 394, National Archives, Washington, D.C.

16. Robert E. Burke, *Olson's New Deal for California* (Berkeley and Los Angeles: University of California Press, 1953), p. 201.

17. For a detailed discussion of western reaction see Morton Grodzins, *Americans Betrayed: Politics and the Japanese Evacuation* (Chicago: University of Chicago Press, 1949), passim.

18. *Congressional Record*, December 15, 1941, pp. 9808-09.

19. Ford to Stimson, January 16, 1942, Record Group 107, National Archives, Washington, D.C.

20. Stimson to Ford, January 26, 1942, Record Group 107, National Archives, Washington, D.C.

21. Stimson to Biddle, January 25, 1942, Record Group 107, National Archives, Washington, D.C.

22. Stetson Conn, "Japanese Evacuation from the West Coast," p. 121.

23. Telephone conversation, De Witt and Bendetsen, January 24, 1942, Record Group 389, National Archives.

24. Warren's testimony, and that of more than a hundred West Coast leaders, may be found in U.S., Congress, House, Select Committee Investigating National Defense Migration (Tolan Committee), Hearings, 77th Cong., 2d sess., parts 29, 30, 31. (Washington, D.C.: Government Printing Office, 1942).

25. The Roberts Report may be most conveniently found in *Pearl Harbor Attack: Hearings Before the Joint Committee on the Investigation of the Pearl Harbor Attack*, part 39, pp. 1-21 (Washington, D.C.: Government Printing Office, 1946). The quotation is from page 12.

26. Biddle, *In Brief Authority*, p. 216.

27. See the mimeographed statement in folder "California Joint Immigration Committee," Robert W. Kenny Manuscripts, Bancroft Library, Berkeley, California.

28. Memorandum, Marshall to General Eisenhower, January 30, 1942, Record Group 107, National Archives, Washington, D.C.

29. Stetson Conn, "The Hawaiian Defenses After Pearl Harbor," pp. 207-210, in Stetson Conn et al., *Guarding the United States.*

3

Citizen and Alien Enemies

The political pressure for mass evacuation really began to build at the end of January, 1942. On January 29, James H. Rowe, one of Biddle's top aides, agreed reluctantly, through Bendetsen, to the removal of all aliens *and* all persons of Japanese descent from Bainbridge Island in Puget Sound. Rowe realized the implications of his agreement. "The only thing that bothers me," he told Bendetsen, "if we agree upon one [area] we might as well admit that we're going to have the problem in every prohibited area, they'll want all Jap citizens out. But anyway I don't know what we can do."[1]

Rowe was only half right. Pressure would grow from the army and navy for the removal of not only enemy aliens but also American citizens of Japanese ancestry (what Rowe called "Jap citizens") from places like Bainbridge and Terminal Island in the Los Angeles harbor area and in the areas around vital war plants, particularly aircraft factories (see Document 6). In addition, however, there would be increasing pressure for the removal of all Japanese from the entire West Coast. *(Alternative 4: Mass Incarceration of West Coast Japanese, Alien and Citizen.)*

On January 27 and 29, De Witt had separate meetings with California's Governor and Attorney General, Culbert Olson and Earl Warren (see Document 6-c). Both agreed, as he reported to Bendetsen, that:

There's a tremendous volume of public opinion now developing against the Japanese of all classes, that is aliens and nonaliens, to get them off the land, and in Southern California around Los Angeles—in that area too—they want and they are bringing pressure on the government to move all the Japanese out. As a matter of fact, it's not being instigated or developed by people who are not thinking but by the best people of California. Since the publication of the Roberts Report they feel that they are living in the midst of a lot of enemies. They don't trust the Japanese, none of them.[2]

"The best people of California," and of other West Coast states as well, were also putting increasing pressure on their elected representatives in Washington. On January 30, Bendetsen, along with Rowe and Edward J. Ennis of the Justice Department, attended a meeting of the California House delegation. Two or three congressmen from Washington state were also present. The group passed a resolution calling for the army to have full control over the enemy aliens programs on the West Coast (the War Department's message that the Justice Department "wasn't functioning" had clearly gotten through) and asking for much more stringent steps than the government had publicly announced.

A recommendation to the President that the War Department be given immediate and complete control over all alien enemies as well as United States citizens holding dual citizenship in any enemy country, with full authority and power to require and direct the cooperation and assistance of all other agencies of the government in exercising such control and in effectuating evacuation, resettlement and internment.

A recommendation to the War Department and other interested agencies that the following program be initiated at once:

1. A designation by the War Department of critical areas throughout the country and territorial possessions.
2. Immediate evacuation of all such critical areas of all enemy aliens and their families, including children under 21 whether aliens or not.
3. Temporary internment of evacuated aliens and families in available CCC camps pending completion of long range resettlement or internment program.
4. Opportunity and federal assistance to dual citizens who live in critical areas for voluntary resettlement and evacuation as a patriotic contribution.
5. Federal assistance to all uninterned alien enemies and dual citizens whose means of livelihood are affected either by execution of the program outlined above or by unemployment brought about by other factors.
6. The development and consummation as soon as possible of a program of complete evacuation and resettlement or internment covering all alien enemies and dual citizens wherever located (see Document 7).

The action of this unofficial congressional caucus, whose members were, in Bendetsen's words, "pretty stirred up," merits some analysis. Even at the end of January, 1942, there was a distinct reluctance to state baldly that they wanted all Japanese, citizen or alien, evacuated. The phrase in point two about "children under 21 whether aliens or not" would include about half of the American citizens of Japanese ancestry. The rest could be included under the phrase "dual citizens," since, by Japanese law, any ethnic Japanese could claim dual citizenship. It is also interesting that the congressmen were still enough depression-oriented to worry about employment. Yet, despite the circumlocutions—the word Japanese does not appear in the resolution—Bendetsen was correct in describing the resolution to his chief as "calling for the immediate evacuation of all Japanese from the Pacific coastal strip."

It is also clear that officers and officials of both the army and the navy, including Undersecretary of the Navy James V. Forrestal, had been lobbying with some friendly congressmen for just such a program. Bendetsen described his own role in a telephone conversation with General De Witt.

They asked me to state what the position of the Department was. I stated that I could not speak for the War Department. . . . They asked me for my own views and I stated that the position of the War Department was this: that we did not seek control of the program, that we preferred it be handled by the civil agencies. However, the War Department would be entirely willing, I believed . . . to accept the responsibility provided they accorded the War Department, and the Secretary of War, and the military commander under him, full authority to require the services of any federal agency, and required that the agency was required to respond.

This delighted De Witt, who had been frustrated by FBI agents and other federal officials insisting on exercising independent judgment. "In other words," he commented to Bendetsen, "Mr. Hoover himself as head of the FBI would have to function under the War Department exactly as he is functioning under the Department of Justice." De Witt was also "glad to see ... that somebody in authority begins to see the problem." Bendetsen agreed and predicted to De Witt that "opinion is beginning to become irresistible, and I think anything you recommend would be strongly backed up ... by the public." Both agreed that no Japanese was trustworthy under any conditions.

"There are going to be a lot of Japs," De Witt insisted, "who are going to say, 'Oh yes, we want to go, we're good Americans and we want to do everything you say,' but those are the fellows I suspect the most." Bendetsen agreed: "The ones who are giving you only lip service are the ones always to be suspected" (See Document 8).

The informal action of the West Coast congressional caucus was forwarded immediately, not to the president but to Secretary of War Stimson, by the chairman of the meeting, Clarence F. Lea, a Democrat from Santa Rosa who had first been elected in 1916 (See Document 8). Stimson did not answer the letter for almost two weeks, but the demands of the congressmen forced the top echelons of the army to consider seriously, for the first time, the problem of what, if anything, ought to be done about the West Coast Japanese. It is important to realize the tremendous responsibilities that the early months of the war had placed on the army's top leadership, as disaster followed disaster. What seemed a major consideration to the men in the provost marshal general's office and De Witt was merely another decision, and not a particularly vital one, to Stimson and Marshall.

The Doctrine of Military Necessity

On January 31 General De Witt had further reactions to the West Coast congressional proposal and telephoned them to Bendetsen in Washington. He did not like many of the qualifications. The whole notion of a compensated, quasi-voluntary evacuation offended him. "I do not feel it is incumbent on this country to be sentimental in this matter," he told Bendetsen. "The very fact that evacuation is necessary eliminates the thought of voluntary or patriotic action on the part of enemy aliens. They should know it is being done as a war measure and treated accordingly." As to who should be moved, De Witt, at this time, did not equivocate. He wanted "all Germans, all Italians who are enemy aliens and all Japanese who are native-born or foreign-born" removed from critical areas as soon as possible. When Bendetsen informed him that Rowe of the Justice Department had suggested a staggered removal from the eighty-eight category "A" areas by nationality, with Japanese being forced to move first, De Witt rejected the notion, protesting that the long lead time given (until February 24) created a period of real danger. De Witt thought "they all ought to go at once. .. We've waited too long as it is. Get them all out" (see Document 8).

On February 1, armed with these informal recommendations, Bendetsen went to a meeting which Attorney General Biddle had convened in his office. Assistant Secretary of War McCloy, seconded by Gullion and Bendetsen, represented the army while Biddle, backed by James Rowe, Edward Ennis (chief of the Aliens Division of the Justice Department) and J. Edgar Hoover represented the civilian viewpoint. The civilian agency, obviously uncomfortable about its increasingly unfavorable public image of being "soft on Japs," and reacting to pressure from Congress and the media, had prepared a press release to be issued jointly by the two departments, like a communique emerging from negotiating sessions between two hostile powers. The key sentence of this proposed press release read: "The Department of War and the Department of Justice are in agreement that the present military situation does not at this time require the removal of American citizens of the Japanese race [from the West Coast]." Although the Justice Department was arguing against a mass evacuation of citizens, it is crucial to note that the opposition was based on expediency, not constitutional principle. Evacuation was not occurring because it was "not at this time" required. Clearly the doctrine of military necessity superseded constitutional guarantees as far as Biddle and his aides were concerned.

The army, however, would have none of it. McCloy and his associates refused to approve the press release until they had consulted General De Witt, and until General De Witt had completed a scheduled meeting with California Governor Olson and Tom Clark. (How such a meeting could affect a presumably military judgment is an interesting question [see Document 8-b].) Additional discussion between the War and Justice Department representatives further clarified the situation. The people in Justice preferred to act only against enemy aliens. They had evolved, however, a fall back position, which would allow the army effectively to exclude all Japanese, regardless of citizenship, from certain areas. These areas would be declared "military areas" and all persons would be required to have permits to remain in them. If then, no permits were issued to Japanese, exclusion could be effected. Attorney General Biddle also made it clear that the Justice Department would have nothing to do with a mass evacuation of citizens; as far as he was concerned the army would have to do it. Biddle's assistant, James Rowe, was mystified about De Witt's position. Gullion and Bendetsen reported, correctly, that the west coast commander had verbally favored mass evacuation. Rowe remembered, from an early January mission to De Witt's headquarters, that the general had characterized mass evacuation as "damned nonsense." In addition, Justice Department representatives pointed out, the only formal requests from De Witt had been his January 24 recommendation for the establishment of the "A" and "B" restricted areas, which Justice had promulgated but not yet put into effect.

There were some heated exchanges toward the close of the meeting. Rowe, apparently the most passionate of the attorney general's men, attacked Bendetsen, argued that many western congressmen were "just nuts" on the subject, and insisted that there was "no evidence whatsoever of any reason for disturbing citizens." Gullion later remembered that he asked the attorney general: "Well, listen, Mr. Biddle, do you mean to tell me that if the Army, the men on the ground, determine it is a military necessity to move citizens, Jap citizens, that you won't help us?" Biddle reiterated that he and his department would not. At this point, still according to General Gullion's account, Assistant Secretary McCloy made his position perfectly clear: "You are putting a Wall Street lawyer in a helluva box," he told the attorney general, "but if it is a question of the safety of the country [and] the Constitution. ... Why the Constitution is just a scrap of paper to me" (see Document 8-c).

This revealing statement made by a senior civilian official clearly reveals the kinds of values that can, all too easily and all too often, come to prevail at the apex of any government. The judgment of individual men becomes more important than due process of law. Such men often come to feel that they, and only they, really understand what is best for the nation, and, under the guise of preserving it from real or imaginary dangers, are prepared to go to almost any lengths to do what they honestly feel is necessary. The shibboleths they use may vary—"military necessity" and "national security" are two that have been used recently—but the process is the same. Individual or group judgment prevails over national law, and the Constitution becomes "a scrap of paper."

Immediately after the meeting, Gullion and Bendetsen made a joint telephone call to De Witt to apprise him of the situation and to get him formally committed to a mass evacuation. As Gullion put it:

Now I might suggest, General, Mr. McCloy was in the conference and he will probably be in any subsequent conference until we decide about this press release, and he has not had the benefit of all the conversations we have had with you,—if you could give us something, not only in conversation but a written thing that we could record, as stating your position, your recommendations and the reasons for your recommendations, that is what they want to know and McCloy also. We weren't able to tell the conference on what you based your recommendations, other than the reasons I suggested, that you had been on the job going up and down [the Coast] and that is what you had concluded (see Document 8-b).

What the Provost Marshal was really telling the West Coast commander was that their out-of-channel telephone conversations had no official standing and that a formal, written recommendation was now required. He was also alerting him to the fact that the civilian leadership of the army was now taking a definite interest. De Witt indicated that he would make written recommendations but that, because of his busy schedule, it would be at least three or four days before he could get around to it. In this conversation, De Witt reaffirmed his support for total evacuation of Japanese Americans, and insisted, quite shortsightedly, that it involved no serious logistical problems. "I haven't gone into the details of it, but Hell, it would be no job as far as the evacuation was concerned to move 100,000 people. .. We could do it in job lots you see. We could take 4,000 or 5,000 a day, or something like that." All three men agreed that the army should not consent to Biddle's proposed press release and that, as De Witt put it, the people in the Justice Department were "trying to cover themselves and lull the populace into a false sense of security."

The California Plan: Intrastate Evacuation

The next day, Sunday, February 2, De Witt had a meeting with Governor Olson, Tom Clark of the Justice Department, and other federal officials including representatives of the Department of Agriculture. At this meeting real concern was expressed about the effect that removal of the Japanese Americans would have on California's agriculture and thus on food production, an important wartime concern. For the first time, an evacuation within California was proposed. It was feared by California leaders that if all Japanese were removed from the state that large numbers of Mexican and black workers would have to be encouraged to come to California to get the crops in. What the "California plan" eventually proposed was that all Japanese be removed from the coastal areas in which most of them lived and placed in camps in the interior valleys of the state, one hundred to one hundred and fifty miles from the seaboard. From these camps labor gangs of men, women and children could emerge by day to work the crops, but be kept under constraint at nightfall. The double appeal of such a plan to some leaders of California agriculture is obvious: in addition to removing Japanese from vital areas it would also provide them with an agricultural labor force that could not strike or move on to more lucrative defense employment. For a time De Witt seemed attracted to this proposal.

Back in Washington another solution that fell short of total removal from the West Coast was under discussion. On February 3, Stimson, McCloy, Gullion and Bendetsen met to discuss the Justice Department's proposed press release and the Japanese American situation in general. At this meeting the discussion focused on the "pass and permit" solution to the problem. McCloy, and particularly Stimson, were most seriously concerned about certain vital military installations. Above all, they were worried about the large aircraft factories, from the Vultee plant in San Diego to the Boeing factories in Seattle, which accounted for a major share of American warplane production. Under this proposal the areas around these installations would be declared military reservations which no one could either live in or enter without a special permit. If, as everyone assumed, no permits whatsoever were issued to persons of the "Japanese race," regardless of citizenship, the constitutional question could have been avoided. Since these areas were never precisely designated, it is not possible to calculate exactly how many Japanese Americans would have been affected, but it is clear that only a minority would have had to move, and that, for the most part, these moves would have been to undesignated areas nearby.

While this meeting was going on, the Chief of Staff, for the first time, directly participated in discussions of the "Japanese problem." In a telephone call apparently made while the meeting between the two secretaries and the

PMG officials was taking place, Marshall attempted to discover just what the west coast commander was up to. What De Witt told General Marshall was significantly at variance with what he had been saying to Gullion and Bendetsen. Whether this represented a temporary change of opinion or whether the cautious De Witt did not at that time wish to be "out in front" on the question is impossible to determine. In any event, he described, cursorily, the "California plan" of Governor Olson, Tom Clark and the Department of Agriculture representatives, and indicated that such a plan might satisfy him. "I've agreed that if [the civilian authorities] can solve the problem of getting them out of the areas limited as the combat zone, that it would be satisfactory. That would take them about 100 to 150 miles from the coast, and they're going to do that I think. They're working on it. . . I'm only concerned with getting them away from around these aircraft factories and other places" (see Document 8-b).

A memorandum of this conversation was apparently furnished to Secretary Stimson during his meeting with Gullion and Bendetsen on February 3. Immediately after that meeting, Assistant Secretary McCloy also got De Witt on the telephone. This conversation very clearly demonstrates that General De Witt, the "man on the spot," was at least partly controlled by civilian authority from Washington, and calls seriously into question the whole notion of "stern military necessity" upon which the later legal defense of the evacuation was predicated. McCloy began by laying down the law.

> The Army, that means you in that area, should not take the position even in your conversations with the political figures out there that it favors a wholesale withdrawal of Japanese citizens and aliens from the Coast, for the reason that it may get us into a number of complications which we have not yet seen the end of. We have about reached the point where we feel that perhaps the best solution of it is to limit the withdrawal to certain prohibited areas. There are so many legal problems involved in discrimination between the native-born Japanese (that is the American citizens), and the aliens, in the first place; and in the second place, there are so many that would be involved in a mass withdrawal, the social and economic consequences would be so great that we would like to go a little slowly on it, and we are a little afraid that if it gets about out there that the Army is taking the position on mass withdrawal, that it may stimulate . . . ."

At that point General De Witt broke in to insist that: "Mr. Secretary . . . I haven't taken any position." However incredible this may sound in view of what we now know about his verbal recommendations to Gullion and Bendetsen, De Witt knew that he had not yet committed himself on paper beyond his January 21 recommendations for setting up restricted areas from which all enemy aliens were to be barred or regulated. De Witt then went on to explain to McCloy the outlines of the "California plan" which he had discussed with Governor Olson and the others. Both McCloy and De Witt seemed to think that such a limited, intrastate evacuation affecting perhaps twenty thousand adults, might solve the problem. De Witt also dictated his proposed changes to the joint Justice-War Department press release which was still under consideration. His proposed language for the crucial sentence was:

The Secretary of War, General De Witt, the Attorney General and the Director of the Federal Bureau of Investigation believe that the steps taken to date for the control of alien enemies has been appropriate and such additional steps to insure this control will be taken in the future as may be found necessary and advisable.

De Witt explained to McCloy that Governor Olson planned to bring prominent Japanese American citizens to his office, and persuade them to cooperate with the "California plan." The possibility of a largely voluntary evacuation was, according to McCloy a "new element," but he was worried about "the bad ones, the ones that are foreign agents, that are sympathetic with Japan, they will not move voluntarily, will they?"

De Witt insisted that the "bad ones" could be taken care of. He also argued that Italian and German enemy aliens were an individual rather than a group problem, but that "out here, Mr. Secretary, a Jap is a Jap to these people now." The West Coast commander also reported that Governor Olson was extremely concerned lest vigilante activity erupt in certain sections of California, and that if there were no government movement of Japanese, the people would take the law into their own hands. McCloy agreed that this was also a concern of officials in Washington, but no documents that I have seen reflect that concern. There had been, in the weeks after Pearl Harbor, a few assaults against Japanese Americans, and a handful of homicides; if there was real concern about vigilante activity, certainly a positive statement about Japanese American loyalty, such as Attorney General Biddle proposed, would have been an appropriate countermeasure, but this was exactly what the army refused to do.

McCloy and De Witt discussed some of the possible ramifications of the "California plan" without coming to any definite conclusion, but there seemed to be general agreement that it was a viable alternative (see Document 8-e). On the following day, February 4, De Witt confirmed his growing support for the "California plan" in a telephone conversation with Bendetsen, who had just been promoted to lieutenant colonel. He also denied that he had ever wanted to evacuate citizens.

I have never on my own initiative recommended a mass evacuation, or the removal of any man, any Jap, other than an alien. In other words I have made no distinction between an alien as to whether he is Jap, Italian or German—that they must all get out of Area A, that is the category A area. The agitation to move all the Japanese away from the coast, and some suggestions, out of California entirely—is within the state, the population of the state, which has been espoused by the Governor. I have never been a body [sic] to that, but I have said, if you do that, and you can solve that problem, it will be a positive step toward the protection of the coast . . . But I have never said, "You've got to do it, in order to protect the coast," . . . I can take such measures as are necessary from a military standpoint to control the American Jap if he is going to cause trouble within those restricted areas (see Document 8-f).

De Witt's contention that he had never recommended a mass evacuation is, of course, absurd. Just two days before, he was telling the PMG people how easy a full evacuation of Japanese would be. The statement does show, however, that McCloy's message about "not taking a stand" had sunk in. The PMG people were disgusted. As Colonel Archer L. Lerch, Gullion's deputy put it, the "decided weakening of General De Witt" is "most unfortunate." As for the "California plan," Lerch considered that it breathed "too much of the spirit of Rotary" and lacked "the necessary cold-bloodedness of War." The PMG's people were cold-blooded. By February 4 Gullion had to acknowledge that "the two Secretaries are against any mass movement. They are pretty much against it. And they are also pretty much against interfering with citizens unless it can be done legally" (see Document 8-c).

Increased Determination by the Military

Despite resistance by his civilian chiefs and the apparent defection of General De Witt, Gullion authorized Bendetsen to draft a plan that would implement mass evacuation. On February 5, in a memorandum to McCloy, the Provost Marshal General stated that on February 1 he had understood from conversations with General De Witt that the West Coast commander had favored mass evacuation. "Since then," Gullion reported, "I have gained the impression that due to representations by Mr. Clark of the Department of Justice and, possibly, because of additional information, General De Witt has changed his position in favor of more lenient treatment involving cooperation with Japanese-American citizen leaders." Gullion, however, refused to change his mind and told the assistant secretary that "such cooperation will be dangerous to rely on and that the delay involved is extremely dangerous." He continued, therefore, to recommend mass evacuation (see Document 9). The next day, February 6, he signed a formal recommendation for mass evacuation and sent it to McCloy.

Gullion's key provision called for mass evacuation to some place outside the Pacific Coast of all Japanese aliens along with "such citizen members of their families as may volunteer for internment"! Most minor children, it was assumed, would "volunteer" to go with their parents. As late as February 6, then, the most rabidly anti-Japanese officers in the army establishment were not yet confident enough of success to recommend formally that American citizens of Japanese ancestry be subject to mass evacuation and incarceration, even though they had been talking about doing just that for weeks. But in the preamble to the memorandum Gullion warned McCloy of the possible consequences of not being stern enough:

If our production for war is seriously delayed by sabotage in the West Coastal states, we shall very possibly lose the war. I have not personally inspected the situation in those states, but from reliable reports from military and other sources, the danger of Japanese inspired sabotage is great. That danger cannot be temporized with. No half-way measures based upon considerations of economic disturbance, humanitarianism, or fear of retaliation will suffice. Such measures will be "too little or too late" (see Document 9-a).

Increased Political Pressure for Evacuation

In addition to the continuing pressure for evacuation that came from the office of the Provost Marshal General, pressures in the media and from politicians at every level began to escalate. The Los Angeles *Times*, on February 2, editorialized that all Japanese Americans were potential enemies. Using a crude biological analogy it insisted that: "A viper is nonetheless a viper wherever the egg is hatched—so a Japanese-American, born of Japanese parents—grows up to be a Japanese, not an American."

Two days later, Governor Culbert Olson of California, in a radio address, told his audience that it was easier to determine loyalty in Germans and Italians than it was in Japanese. He reported, in false information that must have come from General De Witt that "it is known that there are Japanese residents of California who have sought to aid the Japanese enemy by way of communicating information, or have shown indications of preparation for fifth column activities." He also made public, for the first time, the substance of the meetings between himself, General De Witt, Tom Clark and others, and promised that as a result of their deliberations there would soon occur "the movement and placement of the entire adult Japanese population in California at productive and useful employment within the borders of our state, and under surveillance . . . as shall be deemed necessary."

The previous day, Earl Warren, the Attorney General of California and Olson's political rival (Warren would defeat Olson for the governorship in November, 1942) presided over a meeting attended by 150 California law enforcement officers, largely sheriffs and county district attorneys. According to a report of the meeting filed by a federal government official who attended as an observer:

> In his opening remarks Mr. Warren cautioned against hysteria but then proceeded to outline the [Japanese American] situation in such a fashion as to encourage hysterical thinking . . . Mr. [Isidore] Dockweiler, Los Angeles District Attorney . . . asserted that the United States Supreme Court had been packed with leftist and other extreme advocates of civil liberty and that it was time for the people of California to disregard the law, if necessary, to secure their protection. Mr. Dockweiler finally worked himself into such a state of hysteria that he was called to order by Mr. Warren. The meeting loudly applauded the statement that the people of California had no trust in the ability and willingness of the Federal Government to proceed against enemy aliens. One high official was heard to state that he favored shooting on sight all Japanese residents of the state.

Donald Renshaw, the official making this report, was responsible for sampling public opinion and reporting it to Washington. He had noted in late January that "word of mouth discussions continued with a surprisingly large number of people expressing themselves as in favor of sending all Japanese to concentration camps." He also ventured the opinion—which was totally disregarded—that a respected cabinet officer be sent to California to calm the growing public fear about the "Japanese menace."[3]

On February 5, Fletcher Bowron, the Mayor of Los Angeles, further inflamed public opinion with a radio address that focused, not on alien Japanese, but on citizens.

Right here in our city are those who may spring to action at an appointed time in accordance with a prearranged plan wherein each of our little Japanese friends will know his part in the event of any possible invasion or air raid. . . . [Even if] all of the alien Japanese should be placed in concentration camps or evacuated from the coastal area, we would still have with us the more perplexing problem of the American-born Japanese, among whom are unquestionably a number of persons who are loyal to this country—and a number who are doubtless loyal to Japan, waiting probably, to play their part when the time comes.

Bowron claimed that it would be impossible to tell the loyal from the disloyal and argued that

the most natural thing would be for the most dangerous [Japanese Americans] to condemn the Japanese war clique, the Axis powers, to loudly declare a prejudice against Japan and proclaim a belief in American democracy with an emotional pledge of allegiance to the Stars and Stripes. Of course they would try to fool us. They did in Honolulu and in Manila, and we may expect it in California. . . . If we can send our own young men to war . . . it is nothing less than sickly sentimentality to say that we will do injustice to American-born Japanese to merely put them in a place of safety so that they can do no harm. . . . The Japanese problem is centered in Los Angeles, and we are the ones who will be the human sacrifices if the perfidy that characterized the attack on Pearl Harbor is ever duplicated on the American continent. . . . We take our own boys to fight. Let us take the native-born Japanese to serve the government in another way. If they are loyal to this country they could not object; if they are loyal to Japan it would be the best and safest place for them.

Bowron made it clear that he was advocating some version of the "California plan" and envisaged the Japanese being placed on farms or in Civilian Conservation Corps camps. Although he attacked federal officials generally, he made an exception for "Mr. Thomas C. Clarke [sic] of the Department of Justice [who] is going about the great task in a very intelligent way."[4]

The West Coast media continued to help create a regional climate of opinion that was receptive to the demands of the political leaders. On January 29 a federal observer of public opinion had reported, confidentially, that "this week the matter [of mass evacuation] has flared up again in the press with a growing demand that positive action be taken by the Federal Government. This awakening of the press has increased the verbal discussions that never ceased." One of the loudest clamorers had been John B. Hughes, a network radio commentator who was quite harsh in his attacks on public officials, particularly federal officials, asserting that by their inaction, they were exposing the West Coast to real danger. On February 5, a national columnist, Henry McLemore wrote: "Mr. Biddle is the attorney general—but he could run for office in California and not even win the post of third assistant dog catcher. Maybe feeling is wrong. All I know is that Californians have the feeling that he is the one in charge of the Japanese menace, and that he is handling it with all the severity of Lord Fauntleroy."[5]

While this pressure was building up publicly, West Coast congressmen were secretly organizing themselves as a special interest group to force federal action. On February 2 and 3 the Pacific Coast congressional delegation met in House and Senate caucuses to see if they could get results. Senator Hiram W. Johnson, the California progressive Republican warhorse who had been serving in the Senate since 1917, coordinated the efforts of the senators. In the mid-1920s he had masterminded a similar congressional caucus to secure adoption of Japanese exclusion in the Immigration Act of 1924. Although eager for mass evacuation, in 1942 Johnson was more concerned about the defense of the Pacific Coast—he expected a direct Japanese attack—and he complained to one of his chief political lieutenants that "the keenness of interest in the Japanese question far overshadowed the general proposition of our preparedness."[6]

Johnson had not been convinced by arguments which had been presented to the West Coast caucus by a whole array of military brass. Among those who talked to the group were Admiral Harold R. Stark, Chief of Naval Operations, Brigadier General Mark W. Clark of Marshall's staff, and Colonel Hoyt S. Vandenburg. According to the memorandum for record filed by Colonel Wilton B. Persons, Chief of the army's [congressional] Liaison Branch, Senator Rufus B. Holman, an Oregon Republican, was the chief spokesman. He pressed for a rapid mass evacuation, arguing that the people of the West Coast were "alarmed and terrified as to their person, their employment, and their homes." The legislators, who, as we know, had previously received the view of the PMG's men from Bendetsen, were then provided with their first truly military briefing from Mark Clark, who presented the view of the General Staff. Clark insisted that the westerners were "unduly alarmed," and concluded, correctly as we now know, that the Japanese military did not have the capability to make a full-scale attack on the American West Coast. He did admit that an occasional air raid or a commando attack or two were within the range of possibility and that a Japanese attack on Alaska "was not a fantastic idea." This military reassurance was not very convincing to the politicians. After all, the military had been asleep at the switch at Pearl Harbor, and in the weeks since the Japanese military had seemed invincible. Their caucus, therefore, through its Committee on Alien Enemies and Sabotage, continued to press the administration to take action.[7]

These and other pressures apparently began to have their effect on McCloy. On February 7, probably in response to Gullion's memorandum and recommendation of February 5 and 6, he sent Bendetsen back to the West Coast "to confer with General De Witt in connection with mass evacuation of all Japanese." From this point on, McCloy, who had been "pretty much against" mass evacuation earlier in the week, seems to have assumed that mass evacuation would occur. Just what caused him to change his mind does not appear in the record. McCloy has always insisted, publicly, that it was the recommendation from De Witt based on "military necessity" that persuaded him that evacuation had to come. We can now see that the opposite occurred. When it seemed that his views about mass evacuation might get him into trouble with his superiors, De Witt backed down. It was McCloy, accepting the recommendations of the Provost Marshal General, who initiated the final push for mass evacuation. At no time, during the first days of February, when the crucial decisions were made, did General De Witt officially recommend moving American citizens of Japanese ancestry. What he did recommend was a constant broadening of the Category A areas on the West Coast from which all enemy aliens would be barred. Although much was made, then and later, about the allegedly sinister concentration of Japanese aliens around these strategic points, the fact was that De Witt's recommendations, if they had been acted upon, would have moved more German and Italian aliens than Japanese.

By February 9, however, Attorney General Biddle, who had to implement De Witt's recommendations, had just about had enough. In six public announcements between January 29 and February 7, Biddle, following War Department recommendations, had established 135 separate areas in the states of California, Oregon, Washington and Arizona, as "prohibited areas from which all German, Italian, and Japanese alien enemies are to be completely excluded." The effective dates for these exclusions were set for February 15 and 24. In addition, on February 4, the Attorney General announced that "the entire coast line of California from the Oregon border to a point approximately 50 miles north of Los Angeles, and extending inland for distances varying from 30 to 150 miles has been declared a 'restricted area' for all alien enemies" (see Document 10). Within this "restricted" coastal strip, unlike the prohibited areas, enemy aliens could remain but were to be subjected to a 9:00 P.M. to 6 A.M. curfew. At all other times they were to be restricted to their place of residence, their place of employment, or "going between those two places, or within a distance of not more than 5 miles from the place of residence." These proclamations would have affected more German and Italian aliens than Japanese aliens because the city and county of Los Angeles, where most Japanese Americans lived, were not restricted. The restricted area also omitted almost all of the large West Coast aircraft factories which were in San Diego, Los Angeles and Seattle. But Biddle resisted strongly, in conferences and in formal letters, suggestions that the entire county of Los Angeles be made a prohibited area, or that Japanese who were native born citizens be prohibited along with enemy aliens. Biddle insisted to his cabinet colleague, Stimson, that his department had "no power or authority" to evacuate Japanese who were American citizens.

Biddle, however, did agree that there were ways in which this could be done.

The question of whether or not Japanese should be evacuated, whether citizens or not, necessarily involves a judgment based on military considerations. This, of course, is the responsibility of the Army. I have no doubt that the Army can legally, at any time, evacuate all persons in a specified territory if such action is deemed essential from a military point of view for the defense and protection of the area. No legal problems arise when Japanese citizens [i.e., enemy aliens] are evacuated; but American citizens of Japanese origin could not, in my opinion, be singled out of an area and be evacuated with the other Japanese. However the result might be accomplished by evacuating all persons in the area and then licensing back those whom the military authorities thought were not objectionable from a military point of view. These suggestions are made to you for your careful consideration in view of your prior recommendations and of the probable necessity of your taking further vigorous action (see Document 11).

Roosevelt Gives the Army Authority

By the time Biddle signed this letter—February 12—Stimson and McCloy, aware of the position that he would take, had already gone over his head to the White House to request the transfer of some authority over civilian populations from the Department of Justice to the War Department. On February 11, after a conference between Stimson, McCloy and Brigadier General Mark W. Clark of the General Staff, Stimson tried to obtain an appointment with the president. Roosevelt had a full schedule that day, but Stimson—perhaps with McCloy on an extension—talked to the president on the telephone in the early afternoon. Since neither Roosevelt nor Stimson recorded their telephone conversations we cannot know precisely what was said. We do know, from an unsigned memorandum for record of the same date the four alternatives that the War Department wished to place before the Commander in Chief.

1. Would FDR authorize the Army to move American citizens of Japanese anecstry as well as aliens?
2. Should they evacuate the entire West Coast, more than 100,000 people?
3. Should they undertake a large but not total evacuation of the major urban areas, involving perhaps seventy thousand people?
4. Should they restrict themselves to evacuating small areas around critical areas like aircraft factories, even though that would be more complicated and tension-producing than total evacuation? (see Document 11-a).

Franklin Delano Roosevelt refused to choose. According to Assistant Secretary McCloy, who telephoned the good news almost immediately to Bendetsen in San Francisco, the president gave the army *"carte blanche* to do what we want to."* This included, specifically, the authority to evacuate American citizens of Japanese ancestry. The only restriction that Roosevelt placed on the army was that it should "be as reasonable as you can."[8]

Why did Roosevelt do it? No historian can ever answer, definitively, this kind of question, but every historian worth his salt must at least try. Nothing anyone can say in explanation, however, can expiate it; no doctrine of historical relativism can absolve Franklin Roosevelt of the responsibility for giving the army the right to treat American citizens of Japanese ancestry as it wished. But the student of history must also try to understand the forces of history that were at work. Roosevelt, as we have seen, harbored all sorts of racist prejudices against Asians, along with most Americans. In addition, February, 1942, was a particularly bad time for the United States. The Japanese offensive that had begun with the attack on Pearl Harbor in December continued. Imperial forces had landed on the island of

Singapore on February 8, on New Britain on February 9, and were advancing rapidly in Burma. Roosevelt was concerned, first, with winning the war, and second, with unity at home, so that he, unlike Wilson, could win the peace with the advice and consent of the Senate. He could read the congressional signs well, and knew that cracking down on the Japanese Americans would be popular both on Capitol Hill and with the nation at large. And the last thing that he wanted was a rift with establishment Republicans like Stimson and McCloy, despite urgings for restraint from a few of the staunchest New Dealers in his administration. So do what you think you have to do to win the war, he, in effect, told the civilian spokesmen for the military. And one can imagine him on the phone in the great Oval Office where so much of our history has been made, that leonine head lifting up and with the politician's charm and equivocation saying, "Be as reasonable as you can." Thus do great and good men do evil acts in the name of good.

Notes

1. Telephone conversation, Bendetsen and Rowe, January 29, 1942, Record Group 389, National Archives, Washington, D.C.
2. Telephone conversation, Bendetsen and De Witt, January 30, 1942, Record Group 389, National Archives, Washington, D.C.
3. Material on the California meeting and public opinion from the California reports for January and February, 1942, is from the Office of Government Reports, Record Group 44, Washington National Records Center, Suitland, Maryland.
4. Reprinted in *Congressional Record*, February 9, 1942, pp. A547-48.
5. Los Angeles *Times*, January 29, 1942.
6. Hiram W. Johnson to Frank P. Doherty, February 16, 1942, Hiram W. Johnson Manuscripts, Bancroft Library.
7. Memorandum for Record by Person, February 6, 1942, Stetson Conn, "Notes" (personal files).
8. Telephone conversation, McCloy and Bendetsen, February 11, 1942, Stetson Conn, "Notes."

4

"To Hell With Habeas Corpus"

Despite the presidential go-ahead, there was as yet no firm notion within the War Department as to what, exactly, was necessary. At the time, Stimson seems to have felt that a quick evacuation of all Japanese, citizen and alien, from around "the most vital places of army and navy production" would be best. Gullion and Bendetsen continued to want total evacuation of Japanese and seem to have won McCloy to their position. The General Staff, as we shall see, wanted no mass evacuation whatsoever, while General De Witt, caught in the middle, vacillated wildly from position to position.

The Chief of Staff, George C. Marshall, had not been central to most of the discussions and decision making about enemy aliens in general and Japanese Americans in particular. Provost Marshal General Gullion's crucial memorandum of February 6, recommending mass evacuation to the secretary of war, was sent to Marshall only on February 11, the same day that Roosevelt gave the green light to Stimson. There is no evidence that the president ever even asked for Marshall's opinion. That opinion, the real military necessity as seen by the professional head of the army, seems to be best represented in an official memorandum on the subject from one of his key staff subordinates, Brigadier General Mark W. Clark. Noting that General De Witt and "apparently powerful groups on the west coast" were pushing for mass evacuation, Clark, on about February 12, insisted that he could not "agree with the wisdom of such a mass exodus." His reasoning, not in the least influenced by civil libertarian notions or what the PMG people would call "the spirit of Rotary" is worth discussing at length. Clark insisted that there would never be a "perfect defense against sabotage." He thought the situation was analogous to protecting such installations from air attack by means of antiaircraft guns and barrage balloons. Observing that there would never be "enough" of such means, he questioned the efficacy of mass removal as an antidote to sabotage. What frightened Clark was the vast amounts of manpower which the PMG people estimated would be necessary to handle the evacuation—one soldier to every four or five evacuees. He insisted that:

> we must not permit our entire offensive effort to be sabotaged in an effort to protect all establishments from ground sabotage. . . . We must determine what are our really critical military installations, give them thorough protection and leave others to incidental means in the hope that we will not lose too many of them—and above all keep our eye on the ball—that is the creating and training of an offensive army.

Clark's formal proposals were to set up a limited number of critical areas, to eject all enemy aliens from those areas and set up a "pass and permit" system to control the presence of others, leave countersubversive activity to the FBI, and, finally, that "This alien group should be made to understand through publicity that the first overt act on their part will bring a wave of counter-measures which will make the historical efforts of the vigilantes look puny in comparison."[1]

This, then, represented the military judgment. As late as February 12, Clark apparently thought that only a very limited evacuation, along the lines that he had recommended, was going to be effected. In a telephone conversation that day De Witt informed him that he was "putting in a paper" recommending the evacuation of all Japanese from category "A" areas. De Witt was apparently nervous about his past short-circuiting of the chain of command, and told Clark that he was "a little uncertain" as to whether the Chief of Staff had been fully informed of everything. De Witt spoke to Clark of a move that would involve perhaps 60,000 people. But on the previous day, February 11, Colonel Bendetsen, speaking from De Witt's headquarters, had given two different figures to officials in Washington. At 2:15 P.M., Washington time, he had given Assistant Secretary McCloy the figure of 61,000, but a little over an hour later, talking to his chief Gullion, he used the figure of 101,000 people. In this latter conversation it becomes apparent that Stimson was still thinking in terms of creating relatively small "Jap-less" islands around vital defense installations, while McCloy had been converted to the Gullion-Bendetsen view that such a scheme was impractical because, as Bendetsen put it: "Inside of Los Angeles, you have so many industrial installations over the face of the city that if you did attempt to establish a protective island around each of those installations, you would find first that those circles would soon overlap, and also, of course, all the supply lines and power lines. . . ."[2]

At this crucial point, additional political pressures were brought to bear which also favored mass evacuation. On February 12, Walter Lippmann, perhaps the most influential columnist in the nation, published, from San Francisco, a column entitled "The Fifth Column on the Coast." Its major argument was for some kind of mass removal of Japanese, although the columnist laid out no blueprint:

> . . . the Pacific Coast is in imminent danger of a combined attack from within and without. . . . It is a fact that the Japanese navy has been reconnoitering the coast more or less continuously. . . . There is an assumption [in Washington] that a citizen may not be interfered with unless he has committed an overt act. . . . The Pacific Coast is officially a combat zone. Some part of it may at any moment be a battlefield. And nobody ought to be on a battlefield who has no good reason for being there. There is plenty of room elsewhere for him to exercise his rights.

The column drew a great deal of attention. Fellow columnist Westbrook Pegler, who had been calling for concentration camps since early December was delighted to find so respectable an ally; he translated Lippmann's column into the vernacular and rendered it: "The Japanese in California should be under armed guard to the last man and woman right now—and to hell with habeas corpus."[3] It was also widely read in Washington: General Marshall had a copy of Lippmann's column clipped and sent to Stimson, who in turn passed it on to McCloy. It was almost certainly read in the White House as well.

The next day, February 13, the entire Pacific Coast congressional delegation signed and sent to the president a resolution that went much farther than the resolution that some House members had sent to the secretary of war at the end of January. The stronger resolution echoed what Gullion and Bendetsen were calling for by recommending "the immediate evacuation of all persons of Japanese lineage and all others, alien and citizen alike, whose presence shall be deemed dangerous or inimical to the defense of the United States from all strategic areas . . . such areas [should] be enlarged as expeditiously as possible until they shall encompass the entire strategic areas of the states of California, Oregon and Washington, and the Territory of Alaska."[4] The same day, in California, General De Witt, with the assistance of Colonel Bendetsen, finally submitted the recommendations "that Mr. McCloy wanted." His recommendations, for the first time, included a specific written request for the forced evacuation by federal authority of American citizens of Japanese ancestry from the category "A" areas already established by him (see Document 12). This would have meant evacuation from the coastal strip and from strategic areas, but was still consistent with the "California plan" which he, Governor Olson, and Tom Clark had been considering. Clark, for his part, made public assurances to Californians that federal action would be taken to solve the Japanese problem. A February 14 press conference he held in Los Angeles was summarized by the Los Angeles *Times:*

> Emergency orders by the United States Government to evacuate 266,000 enemy aliens and their children, including all American-born Japanese, from areas in California vital to national defense will be recommended [February 15] at a conference in Washington, D.C., by Federal Alien Co-Ordinator Tom C. Clark, he disclosed here yesterday before his departure for the capital.[5]

Again, Clark's statement was fully consistent with the "California plan."

A Last Word of Protest

In Washington, however, Clark's boss, Attorney General Biddle, was making a belated and futile protest against the planned mass evacuation in a letter to the president. When he wrote the letter, on February 17, he was apparently not yet aware that FDR had given the green light to Stimson and McCloy six days previously. Biddle began by noting the "increasing demands for the evacuation of all Japanese" from the West Coast, and specifically cited the columns by Lippmann and Pegler, noting that these spoke of imminent "attack on the West Coast and widespread sabotage." Biddle stated that the War Department expected no attack and that the FBI had "no evidence of planned sabotage." He told the president that he had "designated as a prohibited area every area recommended to me by the War Department" and, somewhat curiously, argued that "there is no dispute between the War, Navy and Justice Departments." In arguing against the evacuation of "93,000 Japanese in California," he stressed expediency. It was unnecessary; it would disrupt agricultural production; "require thousands of troops, tie up transportation and raise very difficult questions of resettlement." Only in passing did the former law clerk to Oliver Wendell Holmes, Jr., and the chief law enforcement officer of the United States mention that "under the Constitution 60,000 of these Japanese are American citizens." His harshest words were reserved for Walter Lippmann:

> It is extremely dangerous for columnists, acting as "Armchair Strategists and Junior G-Men," to suggest that an attack on the West Coast and planned sabotage is imminent when the military authorities and the F.B.I. have indicated that this is not the fact. It seems close to shouting FIRE! in the theater; and if race riots occur, these writers will bear a heavy responsibility. Either Lippman [sic] has information which the War Department and the F.B.I. apparently do not have, or he is acting with dangerous irresponsibility.[6]

Lippmann, of course, did not make these things up. Much of his misinformation apparently came from California Attorney General Earl Warren, who, in turn, had received it from General De Witt. In any event, Biddle's message to the president had no effect; there is no indication that FDR answered it.

The same day Biddle wrote Roosevelt, the PMG's office sent a telegram to every Corps Area commander within the United States alerting them to the "closely guarded secret" that "orders for very large evacuation of enemy aliens of all nationalities predominantly Japanese" would probably be issued within forty-eight hours and asked how many each could accommodate, including "men, women and children" (see Document 13). That afternoon Stimson, McCloy, Gullion, General Mark Clark, and Bendetsen, just back from San Francisco, held a conference to try to thrash out a general timetable for the evacuation. Clark, speaking for the General Staff, protested against the assignment of any additional troops to De Witt for the evacuation. That evening McCloy, seconded by Gullion and Bendetsen, met at Biddle's home with the attorney general and some of his aides. At this meeting Gullion read to the attorney general a proposed executive order he had drafted for the president's signature, which would empower the army to evacuate civilians. By this time the Justice Department had ceased its resistance to the War Department's program.

The Delegation of Presidential Authority

The Executive Order, which Franklin Roosevelt signed on February 19 in the form in which the army sent it to him (see Document 14) was a sweeping, and unprecedented, delegation of presidential power to an appointed subordinate. Although, as it turned out, its authority was used only against Japanese Americans, it was an instrument that could have affected any American. Basing itself on a war powers act passed in 1918, the order empowered the Secretary of War and military commanders designated by him to prescribe "military areas" of unlimited extent "from which any or all persons may be excluded" at the discretion of the commander. The War Department was authorized to provide "such transportation, food, shelter, and other accommodations" as he might deem necessary for persons so evacuated. The jurisdiction of the War Department was made to supersede the authority of the Justice Department in such areas, and all executive departments of the government were directed to assist the military in carrying out any subsequent evacuation.

With the signing of this order, the War Department had the power arbitrarily to evacuate and incarcerate any American. Although only the West Coast situation was discussed in connection with the order, Gullion had shrewdly designed it so that it could be applied against any group anywhere in the country. No geographical areas were specified, no ethnic groups mentioned, and no distinctions made between citizen and alien.

The president's signature, therefore, while giving great potential power to the army, did not, in and of itself, single out any one group or person for evacuation. Before that could happen, Secretary Stimson had to delegate the power given him to a subordinate commander and to draft instructions for that commander. There was still debate within the executive branch as to how much of the authority should be used and against whom. As we have seen, some were still thinking about creating "Jap-less islands" in California and moving perhaps 60,000 people, some were thinking about moving out the total Japanese population—about 110,000 people—and some, like Tom Clark, had talked about moving all Japanese and all enemy aliens, some 266,000 people. There was also debate about whether to move people within the state—the "California plan"—or to get them east of the Sierra Nevada, as the PMG people proposed. There was disagreement about who should be responsible for the custody of the people, once they were moved. The PMG people, involved in empire building, wanted continuing jurisdiction over all enemy aliens, while the General Staff, jealous of its manpower, wanted a minimum of military personnel involved.

The War Department continued to get conflicting advice from California. On February 20, for example, Carey McWilliams, chief of Governor Olson's Division of Immigration and Housing and later one of the most important journalistic critics of the evacuation, wired the attorney general suggesting, in essence, a modified "California plan" and recommending the establishment of an "Alien Control Authority" to be composed of both military and civilian representatives of the federal government. The War Department did not heed this advice, but neither did it follow the counsel of its "man on the spot," General De Witt. The West Coast commander's February 13 recommendations—which arrived in Washington late on February 18—called for the evacuation of all Japanese and all German and Italian aliens from the following locations, which he proposed to declare military areas (see Document 14-a).

    a. San Diego
    b. Los Angeles

c. San Francisco, including the entire bay district

d. The portion of Washington lying west of the Cascade Mountains

e. The northwest portion of Oregon lying west of the Cascade Mountains

f. A strip alone the Pacific Coast fifteen miles deep

General De Witt estimated that this would involve 133,000 people: about 69,000 Japanese (25,000 aliens and 44,000 citizens), 44,000 Italian aliens and 20,000 German aliens. Although these figures are almost certainly too small, given the areas De Witt intended to clear (and there is no telling, what he might have called for next once having achieved that), it is important to note that De Witt formally proposed a less than total evacuation of Japanese and suggested moving almost as many Europeans as Asians.

The General Staff, apparently not apprised of the decisions that Stimson and McCloy had already made, formally decided on February 19 not to concur in General De Witt's recommendations and recommended, instead, that only enemy alien leaders be arrested and interned, although, presumably, this had already been done by the FBI. The following day, however, probably having been made aware of the real situation by Mark Clark, General Headquarters transmitted De Witt's recommendations through channels with the annotation that they were being sent "in view of the proposed action by the War Department."

On February 20, War Secretary Stimson formally designated De Witt as "the Military Commander to carry out the duties and responsibilities imposed" by Roosevelt's Executive Order for the Western Defense Command (see Document 14-b). Stimson's letter instructed De Witt not to undertake mass removals of Italian aliens or persons of Italian lineage and "suggested" that it might be necessary for De Witt to exempt Italian aliens from the attorney general's regulations already published. De Witt was also forbidden to use troops of two infantry divisions training in his command to effect the evacuation. De Witt was instructed to go slowly, to clear everything with Washington first, to cause as little disruption of commerce and industry as possible, and to insure, wherever possible, that "fullest advantage should be taken of the voluntary exodus of individuals."

Assistant Secretary McCloy, who now took full charge of the Washington end of evacuation and relocation planning, sent even more detailed instructions to De Witt the same day in a five-page "Outline Memorandum" (see Document 14-c). This spelled out the briefer instructions in Stimson's letter. The two documents, taken together, demonstrate clearly that in the final analysis, Washington and not De Witt's Western Defense Command made the crucial decisions. The memorandum discussed five categories of individuals subject to exclusion: Japanese aliens, Japanese citizens, German aliens, Italian aliens, and, persons who, regardless of citizenship status, were suspected of being dangerous. As in Stimson's letter, chief priority was given to Japanese, regardless of citizenship status, and to German aliens. The memorandum, however, directed De Witt to make exception for "bona fide refugees" who were German aliens, and suggested that persons over seventy "should not be disturbed except for good and sufficient reasons." Neither

Stimson's letter nor the "Outline Memorandum" specified when mass evacuation would begin, where evacuees would be confined, or who would be in charge of them.

Decisions on Evacuation Procedures

A cabinet meeting on February 27 settled one of these problems. It was decided that some individual, a civilian, would be placed in charge of all resettlement. On March 18 Executive Order 9102 established a new federal agency, the War Relocation Authority (WRA), to handle resettlement. A Department of Agriculture bureaucrat, Milton S. Eisenhower, was appointed as its head. Eventually a division of labor was worked out so that the army was responsible for rounding up the persons to be evacuated and bringing them to staging areas, called Assembly Centers, while the new WRA was responsible for the operation and maintenance of the camps where the evacuees were "permanently" housed. These camps were given small military guard units, but the heavy manpower drain, which had alarmed the General Staff, was avoided. Fewer than two thousand military personnel were detailed to the "permanent" guard detachments.

By late February and early March congressional and public opinion again made themselves felt and helped shape evacuation policy. An already established committee of the House of Representatives, the Select Committee Investigating National Defense Migration, headed by John Tolan, a California Democrat, held hearings in major West Coast cities and filed official recommendations. The testimony they heard almost universally favored mass evacuation of Japanese regardless of citizenship—some witnesses favored mass deportation after the war—but protested vehemently against mass evacuation of either Italian or German aliens. The general tenor of the testimony was that most of the individuals in the latter groups were loyal and that it was possible to determine loyalty or disloyalty on an individual basis. After hearing a number of witnesses, the committee came to agree.

Its key recommendations were two: Japanese should not be allowed to run loose and German and Italian aliens should be examined individually. Evacuation policy eventually came to reflect closely these congressional recommendations, although, it must be noted that even before the committee took the matter up the War Department had given evidence of having misgivings about moving large numbers of Caucasian enemy aliens. By the end of March (see Document 15) General De Witt was forced to issue a proclamation which, in effect, exempted Germans and Italians from the consequences of his orders, but he continued to believe that all enemy aliens should be moved out. In May, for example, he complained to Bendetsen that: "I'm definitely of the opinion that the original Proclamation should stand, that after we finish the Japs we take up the Germans and then the Italians. . . ." [7]

On March 2, General De Witt, superseding the authority of the attorney general under Roosevelt's Executive Order, issued Public Proclamation No. 1.

As "a matter of military necessity" the West Coast states and Arizona were divided into two military zones. Military Area No. 1 comprised roughly the eastern half of Washington, Oregon and California and the southern half of Arizona. Military Area No. 2 comprised the rest of those states. In addition, ninety-nine special zones were established within both areas which corresponded roughly to the areas previously declared restricted by the attorney general, including a strip about fifteen miles wide running the entire length of the coast and along the Mexican border. In this proclamation, for the first time, restrictions were applied not only to "any Japanese, German or Italian alien" but also to "any person of Japanese Ancestry." While the proclamation did not move anyone, it did order all affected persons living in Military Area No. 1 to file an official notice with the post office if he was going to move. In addition, the proclamation encouraged affected individuals to move voluntarily into Military Area No. 2, where, presumably, they would be left in peace.

One of the reasons, perhaps, that this and other early proclamations did not impose any regulations on the affected classes was that Gullion's office had become aware, late in February, that there were no penalties in law for a civilian who disobeyed a military order. Accordingly, a statute creating this new federal crime was drafted in the War Department and sent to Congress on March 9. The next day it was dropped into the hopper by John M. Costello, a friendly California Democrat on the House Committee on Military Affairs. It was reported out a week later, passed both houses without a dissenting vote on March 19, and was signed into law on March 21. The only member of Congress who questioned it at all was Republican Senator Robert A. Taft of Ohio, who called it:

> the 'sloppiest' criminal law I have ever read or seen anywhere. I certainly think the Senate should not pass it. . . . It does not apply only to the Pacific coast. It applies anywhere in the United States where there is any possible reason for declaring a military zone. . . . I have no doubt an act of that kind would be enforced in wartime. I have no doubt that in peacetime no man could ever be convicted under it, because the court would find that it was so indefinite and so uncertain that it could not be enforced under the Constitution.

Yet, because Taft understood "the pressing character of this kind of legislation for the Pacific Coast today," he did not formally object to the measure despite his dislike of it.[8] The new act made any civilian who violated a military order in a military area subject to a year in jail and a $5,000 fine.

Three days after the enactment of the War Department's bill, De Witt issued his first restrictive proclamation (see Document 15-a). This imposed an 8:00 P.M. to 6:00 A.M. curfew on all enemy aliens and persons of Japanese ancestry within Military Area No. 1 (where most of the latter lived), restricted their movements to their place of residence, their place of employment, or within five miles of their residence, and prohibited them from possessing firearms, ammunition, explosives, short wave radios, or cameras. The proclamation also stated that, at some future time, certain classes of persons would be entitled to apply for exemption from the restrictions. In point of fact, although many German and Italian aliens did obey the orders, there was no concerted attempt to enforce it except against Japanese.

On the same day, March 24, General De Witt issued his first "civilian exclusion order," significantly numbered "1" (see Document 15-b). It affected Bainbridge Island in Puget Sound, ten miles west of Seattle, and applied only to "persons of Japanese ancestry, including aliens and non-aliens." The Bainbridge Islanders—there were fifty-four families of Japanese fishermen living there—were not the first Japanese to be forced to move by the government. Another fishing community on Terminal Island in the San Pedro, Los Angeles County harbor area, had been moved somewhat capriciously by the navy in February. On the fourteenth of that month the navy had simply posted notices that it was taking over—some five hundred Japanese families lived there—and that all Japanese would have to leave within thirty days, by March 14. But, on the afternoon of February 25, other notices had been posted saying that the deadline had been advanced to midnight, February 27, a little over forty-eight hours away. The Terminal Islanders were, in essence, evicted, and the navy did not care where they went as long as they left the strategic island which abutted vital naval and harbor installations. Most of the Terminal Islanders remained within Los Angeles County.

The Bainbridge Islanders, however, were used as guinea pigs by the army in a kind of dress rehearsal for the full scale evacuation which was to come. De Witt had set up, on March 11, a new military-civilian agency under his command, the Wartime Civil Control Administration (WCCA), and Gullion's man, Karl R. Bendetsen, had been detached from the army staff and promoted to colonel to head it. Tom Clark was loaned to the agency by the Justice Department to be head of its civilian staff. De Witt's proclamation gave the Bainbridge Islanders five days to move "to any approved place beyond the limits of Military Area No. 1." Those who had not moved by March 29—and this was almost all of them—were to be evacuated "in such manner and to such a place or places as shall then be prescribed." According to the "Special Instructions" issued by De Witt to the Bainbridge Islanders, which became standard procedure, those who were being evacuated could bring with them only "that which can be carried" including:

1. Blankets and linens
2. Toilet articles
3. Clothing
4. Sufficient eating utensils including knives, forks, spoons, plates, bowls and cups.

The Decision: Forced Mass Evacuation Of All Japanese

The Bainbridge Islanders at least had the theoretical option of moving voluntarily to an approved place of their choosing. They were the last Japanese Americans in Military Area No. 1 to have that option. While their evacuation was still in progress, on March 27, De Witt issued Public Proclamation No. 4 (see Document 15-c) which stated that "in order to provide for the welfare and to insure the orderly evacuation and resettlement of Japanese voluntarily migrating from Military Area No. 1," no person of Japanese ancestry who was still within the limits of Military Area No. 1 at midnight, March 29 (then a little over forty-eight hours away) could move voluntarily. Thus, at the end of March, the possibility of voluntary evacuation ended for most of the West Coast Japanese.

The whole question of voluntary evacuation has been badly misunderstood. Governmental officials were soon partially to justify the mass evacuation which the Bainbridge Islanders began by arguing that the voluntary evacuation had failed, and some historians and other writers on the evacuation continue to echo this remark. For most of the Japanese Americans, voluntary evacuation was just not a viable alternative. If the head of the family was an alien, his bank account and other funds had been frozen by the federal government. In addition, the area outside of California was *terra incognita* to most of the Japanese Americans and they were naturally reluctant to leave a hostile but known environment for perhaps an even more hostile, unknown one. In addition, some of those who had the means and the nerve to move, encountered mass hostility. In Nevada, for example, vigilante mobs forced several car loads of migrating Japanese to return to California and in Wyoming some were taken into custody by the state police. There were some successful moves: the fully acculturated, American born leaders of the major Japanese American organization (the Japanese American Citizens League, for example) managed to reach the sanctuary of Salt Lake City before the freeze went into effect. Only a small fraction of the Japanese American population managed to effect a move—the official estimates (really guesses) range from two thousand to nine thousand. The majority of these, like the Terminal Islanders, seem to have moved within the states in which they already lived, from Military Area No. 1 to Military Area No. 2, assuming, innocently, that the distinction made by General De Witt in his initial proclamation was a meaningful one. As it turned out, it was not. The evacuation, which started at Bainbridge Island on March 29, proceeded, area by area, to include the entire extent of the three West Coast states, the territory of Alaska, and the southern half of Arizona.

The Bainbridge Islanders were shipped off to a hastily constructed Assembly Center set up by the army at the Washington State Fairgrounds at Puyallup; eventually they were sent to one of the ten, barbed-wire enclosed, army-guarded "Relocation Centers" established by the War Relocation Authority in desolate locations from eastern California to Arkansas. Some of them remained behind barbed wire until the spring of 1946.

The Bainbridge Island dress rehearsal over, Bendetsen and his staff systematically divided the rest of the area to be evacuated into 107 additional areas of quite unequal size, but each with approximately one thousand resident Japanese. A special exclusion order was drafted for each, seriatim, published in the press and posted in the area itself usually one week prior to its effective date. In this manner, the entire West Coast (plus southern

Arizona and Alaska) was gradually cleared of Japanese. By June 5, Military Area No. 1 had been completely cleared; by August 7 the same process had been applied to Military Area No. 2, from which De Witt had stated in his first proclamation on March 2 no evacuation was contemplated.

There was never a mass movement of German and Italian enemy aliens. This policy was never formally enunciated; they simply were not affected by the 108 civilian exclusion orders which uniformly specified Japanese. Nor were some of the inhibitions originally suggested by the War Department with regard to Japanese ever taken into account. Although it had been suggested that it would not be necessary to "disturb" persons over seventy years of age, the civilian exclusion orders made no distinction as to age, sex or, of course, citizenship. Even orphanages run by Caucasian Catholic priests were examined by the army and infant children of partial Japanese ancestry were, in some instances, evacuated. The only exceptions made were for persons who were actually hospitalized; if they later recovered enough to be discharged from the hospital, they, too were evacuated.

In the middle of June, 1942, Assistant Secretary of War John J. McCloy dictated a memorandum for his files reflecting on it all.

> I wonder if anyone realizes the skill, speed and humanity with which the evacuation of the Japanese has been handled by the Army on the West Coast? I am struck with the extreme care that has been taken to protect the persons and goods and even the comforts of each individual. Certainly an organization that can do a humane job like this and still be a fine fighting organization is unique—and American. I hope other countries that have similar problems will not overlook how an answer has been found in this country.[9]

Afterthoughts and Consequences

Few would now agree with McCloy's self-serving appreciation of the military's role in the evacuation. The mass removal and incarceration of the West Coast Japanese was little opposed in 1942, but before the war had come to an end, more and more Americans had come to question its wisdom. Perhaps the turning point, as far as informed public opinion was concerned, came in August, 1945, when Eugene V. Rostow, a legal scholar at Yale, published in *Harper's Magazine* a scathing analysis of the whole affair, calling it "our worst wartime mistake." Since that time, fewer and fewer public voices have been heard in its support. But, despite this widespread regret, the evacuation remains as a dangerous precedent—some might call it a loaded gun—awaiting only an appropriate "crisis" that might evoke a similar response from a frightened or power-seeking government. To understand the parameters of the possibilities, it will be necessary for us to look beyond the decision itself.[10]

The Supreme Court of the United States had three separate chances to declare the evacuation unconstitutional, but, in *Hirabayashi v. U.S.*, in May, 1943, and in *Korematsu v. U.S.* and *Ex parte Endo*, both decided in December, 1944, the Court, in essence, left the evacuation process untouched. Justice William O. Douglas epitomized the spirit of the decisions when he wrote, in *Hirabayashi*, that "we cannot sit in judgment on the military requirements of that hour."[10]

The Court thus left on the historical and legal record what amounted to an approval of the entire evacuation, relocation and detention procedure. As far as American law is concerned, such an incarceration could occur again merely by the issuance of an executive order. There would, of course, have to be an emergency, and there would have to be an acceptable target group. In 1950 it seemed to an overwhelming majority of both houses of Congress that both the emergency and the group existed. At perhaps the height of the Cold War and just subsequent to our involvement in the Korean War, Congress passed over the veto of President Harry S. Truman, the "Emergency Detention Act of 1950" (see Document 16). In a procedure that was patently imitative of the process whereby 110,000 Japanese Americans were herded into concentration camps, this law called upon the government to erect camps

> For the detention of persons who there is reasonable grounds to believe will commit or conspire to commit espionage or sabotage. . . .

All that it took to set the process in motion was the formal declaration by the president of an "Internal Security Emergency," which could be created, according to the statute, by an invasion, a declaration of war or an insurrection within the United States. The statute called for the president to delegate authority to a cabinet officer—the attorney general—who could, presumably, as Stimson did, redelegate that authority. For a time several camps were kept on a standby basis—just to make the analogy even better one of them was at Tule Lake, California, which had previously served as a Relocation Center for Japanese Americans—until the repeal of the statute in 1971. The campaign for its repeal was led by two of the three Japanese Americans then in Congress, Senator Daniel Inouye and Representative Spark Matsunaga, both Democrats from Hawaii. Although Richard Nixon's Justice Department agreed to the repeal, it did so reluctantly (see Document 17). And although no admirer of the American Constitution can regret the repeal of the Emergency Detention Act, it should be remembered that the first mass detention of American citizens on American soil occurred at a time when no federal statute specifically authorized it. However much one may hope that the relocation of the Japanese Americans is buried in the American past, it may yet, in another form, become a part of the American future.

Notes

1. For a longer excerpt, see Roger Daniels, *Concentration Camps, U.S.A.: Japanese Americans and World War II* (New York: Holt, Rinehart and Winston, 1972), pp. 65-67.

2. Telephone conversation, Bendetsen and Gullion, February 11, 1942, Stetson Conn, "Notes" (personal files).

3. Washington *Post*, February 15, 1942, reprinted in *Congressional Record*, February 17, 1942, pp. 568-69.

4. There is a copy of the recommendations in Record Group 107, National Archives, Washington, D.C.

5. Los Angeles *Times*, February 15, 1942.

6. Biddle to FDR, February 17, 1942, Franklin D. Roosevelt Library, Hyde Park, New York.

7. Telephone conversation, De Witt and Bendetsen, May 12, 1942, Record Group 398, National Archives, Washington, D.C.

8. *Congressional Record,* March 19, 1942, p. 2726. The act may be found in U.S. *Statutes at Large,* vol. 56, p. 173.

9. Memorandum for Files, June 15, 1942, Record Group 107, National Archives, Washington, D.C.

10. The three cases are: *Hirabayashi v. U.S.,* 320 U.S. 81; *Korematsu v. U.S.,* 323 U.S. 214; and *Ex parte Endo,* 323 U.S. 283. The literature on these cases is enormous; for an analysis see Chapter 7, "The Court Approves," pp. 130-143 in Daniels, *Concentration Camps, U.S.A.,* and the references cited there.

Part two

Documents of the Decision

1

A
Presidential
Proclamation

Document 1†

By the President of the United States of America
A Proclamation—No. 2525

[Dec. 7, 1941]

AUTHORITY

WHEREAS it is provided by section 21 of title 50 of the United States Code as follows:

"Whenever there is a declared war between the United States and any foreign nation or government, or any invasion or predatory incursion is perpetrated, attempted, or threatened against the territory of the United States by any foreign nation or government, and the President makes public proclamation of the event, all natives, citizens, denizens, or subjects of the hostile nation or government, being of the age of fourteen years and upward, who shall be within the United States and not actually naturalized, shall be liable to be apprehended, restrained, secured, and removed as alien enemies. The President is authorized in any such event, by his proclamation thereof, or other public act, to direct the conduct to be observed, on the part of the United States, toward the aliens who become so liable; the manner and degree of the restraint to which they shall be subject and in what cases, and upon what security their residence shall be permitted, and to provide for the removal of those who, not being permitted to reside within the United States, refuse or neglect to depart therefrom; and to establish any other regulations which are found necessary in the premises and for the public safety."

and

WHEREAS by section 22, 23, and 24 of title 50 of the United States Code further provision is made relative to alien enemies:

PROCLAMATION

NOW, THEREFORE, I, FRANKLIN D. ROOSEVELT, as President of the United States and as Commander in Chief of the Army and Navy of the United States, do hereby make public proclamation to all whom it may concern that an invasion has been perpetrated upon the territory of the United States by the Empire of Japan.

†From: U.S., Congress, House, The Select Committee Investigating National Defense Migration (Tolan Committee), 77th Cong., 2d Sess., 1942, H. Rept. 2124.

CONDUCT TO BE OBSERVED BY ALIEN ENEMIES

And, acting under and by virtue of the authority vested in me by the Constitution of the United States and the said sections of the United States Code, I do hereby further proclaim and direct that the conduct to be observed on the part of the United States toward all natives, citizens, denizens, or subjects of the Empire of Japan being of the age of fourteen years and upwards who shall be within the United States or within any territories in any way subject to the jurisdiction of the United States and not actually naturalized, who for the purpose of this Proclamation and under such sections of the United States Code are termed alien enemies, shall be as follows:

All alien enemies are enjoined to preserve the peace towards the United States and to refrain from crime against the public safety, and from violating the laws of the United States and of the States and Territories thereof; and to refrain from actual hostility or giving information, aid, or comfort to the enemies of the United States or interfering by word or deed with the defense of the United States or the political processes and public opinions thereof; and to comply strictly with the regulations which are hereby or which may be from time to time promulgated by the President.

All alien enemies shall be liable to restraint, or to give security, or to remove and depart from the United States in the manner prescribed by Sections 23 and 24 of Title 50 of the United States Code, and as prescribed in the regulations duly promulgated by the President.

DUTIES AND AUTHORITY OF THE ATTORNEY GENERAL
AND THE SECRETARY OF WAR

And, pursuant to the authority vested in me, I hereby charge the Attorney General with the duty of executing all the regulations hereinafter contained regarding the conduct of alien enemies within continental United States, Puerto Rico, the Virgin Islands and Alaska, and the Secretary of War with the duty of executing the regulations which are hereinafter set forth and which may be hereafter adopted regarding the conduct of alien enemies in the Canal Zone, the Hawaiian Islands, and the Philippine Islands. Each of them is specifically directed to cause the apprehension of such alien enemies as in the judgment of each are subject to apprehension or deportation under such regulations.

REGULATIONS

And, pursuant to the authority vested in me, I hereby declare and establish the following regulations which I find necessary in the premises and for the public safety:

. . . .

(5) No alien enemy shall have in his possession, custody, or control at any time or place or use or operate any of the following enumerated articles:

a. Firearms.

b. Weapons or implements of war or component parts thereof.

c. Ammunition.

d. Bombs.

e. Explosives or material used in the manufacture of explosives.

f. Short-wave radio receiving sets.

g. Transmitting sets.

h. Signal devices.

i. Codes or ciphers.

j. Cameras.

k. Papers, documents or books in which there may be invisible writing; photograph, sketch, picture, drawing, map, or graphical representation of any military or naval installations or equipment or of any arms, ammunition, implements of war, device, or thing used or intended to be used in the combat equipment of the land or naval forces of the United States or of any military or naval post, camp, or station.

All such property found in the possession of any alien enemy in violation of the foregoing regulations shall be subject to seizure and forfeiture.

(6) No alien enemy shall undertaken any air flight or ascend into the air in any airplane, aircraft, or balloon of any sort, whether owned governmentally, commercially or privately, . . .

(7) Alien enemies deemed dangerous to the public peace or safety of the United States by the Attorney General or Secretary of War, as the case may be, are subject to summary apprehension. . . . Alien enemies arrested shall be subject to confinement in such place of detention as may be directed by the officers responsible for the execution of these regulations and for the arrest, detention, and internment of alien enemies in each case, or in such other places of detention as may be directed from time to time by the Attorney General, with respect to continental United States, Alaska, Puerto Rico, and the Virgin Islands, and by the Secretary of War with respect to the Canal Zone, the Hawaiian Islands, and the Philippine Islands, and there confined until he shall have received such permit as the Attorney General or the Secretary of War, with respect to the Canal Zone, the Hawaiian Islands, and the Philippine Islands, shall prescribe.

(8) No alien enemy shall land in, enter or leave or attempt to land in, enter or leave the United States, except under the regulations prescribed by the President in his Proclamation dated November 14, 1941, and the regulations promulgated thereunder or any proclamation or regulation promulgated hereafter.

(9) Whenever the Attorney General of the United States, with respect to the continental United States, Alaska, Puerto Rico and the Virgin Islands, or the Secretary of War, with respect to the Canal Zone, the Hawaiian Islands, and the Philippine Islands, deems it to be necessary, for the public safety and protection, to exclude alien enemies from . . . any locality in which residence by an alien enemy shall be found to constitute a danger to the public peace and safety of the United States . . . , then no alien enemy shall be found within such area or the immediate vicinity thereof. Any alien enemy found

within any such area or the immediate vicinity thereof prescribed by the Attorney General or the Secretary of War, as the case may be, pursuant to these regulations, shall be subject to summary apprehension and to be dealt with as hereinabove prescribed.

(10) With respect to the continental United States, Alaska, Puerto Rico, and the Virgin Islands, an alien enemy shall not change his place of abode or occupation or otherwise travel or move from place to place without full compliance with any such regulations as the Attorney General of the United States may, from time to time, make and declare; . . .

(12) No alien enemy shall enter or be found in or upon any highway, waterway, airway, railway, railroad, subway, public utility, building, place or thing not open and accessible to the Public generally, and not generally used by the public.

(13) No alien enemy shall be a member or an officer of, or affiliated with, any organization, group or assembly hereafter designated by the Attorney General, nor shall any alien enemy advocate, defend, or subscribe to the acts, principles or policies thereof, attend any meetings, conventions, or gatherings thereof or possess or distribute any literature, propaganda or other writings or productions thereof.

FRANKLIN D. ROOSEVELT.

By the President:

CORDELL HULL,
Secretary of State.

NOTE: Proclamations No. 2526 and 2527, Dec. 8, 1941, stated that "an invasion or predatory incursion" was threatened by Germany and Italy and applied the regulations promulgated above to German and Italian nationals.

2

Intramilitary Memos on the Alien Situation

Document 2†

HEADQUARTERS FOURTH ARMY
Presidio of San Francisco, Calif.
G-2

December 11, 1941.

MEMORANDUM TO: Chief of Staff:

1. In compliance with orders of the Chief of Staff received shortly after 10:00 PM, December 10, 1941, I attended a conference of G-2, G-3, G-4 Officers at the headquarters of the Ninth Corps Area.

Present: Colonel O.R. MEREDITH, Chief of Staff.
(For a part of the conference)
Lt. Colonel J.H. WILSON, G-2
Lt. Colonel J.T. ZELLARS, G-3
Lt. Colonel W.S. CONROW, G-4
Captain PASH, Asst. G-2

2. The conference was called by the Corps Area Commander to consider certain questions relative to the problem of apprehension, segregation, and detention of Japanese in the San Francisco Area. The alleged immediate necessity for this segregation was a report by Treasury Agents that an estimated 20,000 Japanese in the San Francisco metropolitan area were ready for organized action.

3. The conference discussed the advisability of taking measures to prevent concerted action by this large group of aliens simultaneously with a possible Japanese landing on the Pacific Coast and sabotage or fifth columnist activities.

4. Three questions were presented by the Corps Area Commander. See Inclosure No. 1 for the questions and their answers by the conference. A brief plan was agreed upon. See Inclosure No. 2.

5. The group then took the plan to General Benedict who approved it generally. However, it was then decided to call the F.B.I. for a definite expression of opinion and the F.B.I. Chief, Mr. Pieper, scoffed at the whole affair as the wild imaginings of a discharged former F.B.I. man named ——. His opinion is included in Inclosure No. 3 as are the remarks of General Benedict.

†From: Record Group 394, National Archives, Washington, D.C.

6. *Conclusion:* The matter as it now stands is looked upon as a closed incident with the exception of the reporting of Mr. Pieper's views to Washington. General Benedict believes however that it may have the effect of arousing the War Department to some action looking to the establishment of an area or areas for the detention of aliens.

JOHN WECKERLING
Lt. Col., Infantry
Asst. A.C. of S., G-2

Document 2-a†

January 1, 1942

MEMORANDUM for the Files.

At 12:15 p.m., January 1, 1942, I took a call from General DeWitt for General Gullion, in the office of General Crawford. General DeWitt stated that his call was prompted by the fact that he had expected Major Bendetsen to arrive and he had not seen him; that the answer had been forthcoming since his call had been put in by the receipt of a radiogram stating that Bendetsen had been grounded at Little Rock and was proceeding by train. However, he stated that he had another question he would like to ask. He asked if the Department of Justice was sending anyone to the Pacific Coast on the alien enemy situation. I told him that Mr. Rowe was leaving tonight by airplane. He asked me who Mr. Rowe was. I told him that he was formerly one of the six confidential secretaries to the President and now an assistant to The Attorney General, considered to be one of the five ranking men in the Department of Justice.

I told him that at a conference yesterday, attended by Mr. McCloy, General Gullion, Mr. Bundy, Mr. Ennis and Mr. Rowe, the representatives of the Department of Justice were very apologetic with reference to their manner of handling alien enemies on the Pacific Coast and had promised to do better; that Bendetsen was carrying with him a copy of a proposed amendment to the Executive Order which would place in the hands of the Secretary of War and such theater commanders as the Secretary of War might designate, the power to control the alien enemy situation. I told him also that while Bendetsen would probably inform him that the amendment was being processed, General Gullion felt that in view of the conference yesterday it would be only fair to the Department of Justice to withhold action on the proposed amendment until we had an opportunity to observe the results of the promises made yesterday by the Department of Justice. General DeWitt had no further questions or comments.

ARCHER L. LERCH,
Colonel, J.A.G.D.,
The Deputy Provost Marshal General.

†From: Record Group 389, National Archives, Washington, D.C.

3

Exclusion of All Alien Enemies from Prohibited Areas

Document 3†
No. 6.   [For immediate release January 29, 1942.]

Department of Justice

Attorney General Francis Biddle announced today that under authority of the Presidential proclamations of December 7 and 8, 1941, controlling alien enemies, a number of areas on the west coast are being designated as prohibited areas from which all German, Italian, and Japanese alien enemies are to be completely excluded.

These prohibited areas have been recommended for selection by the War Department after weeks of careful study under the personal direction of Lt. Gen. J.L. DeWitt, commanding officer, Fourth Army and Western Defense Command. These recommendations were submitted to the Attorney General on Sunday, January 25, by the Secretary of War.

The recommendations so far submitted pertain only to prohibited areas in the State of California. The War Department has advised the Attorney General that further recommendations for other areas in California and in other States in the Western Defense Command will be submitted shortly.

Prohibited area No. 19 (the designation of the War Department) including part of the San Francisco water front in general covers the Embarcadero from pier No. 46 to pier No. 14, and the entire water front from China Basin to the Presidio Reservation boundary line. Area No. 33 in Los Angeles is a rectangle which includes the Municipal Airport and is bounded by the shore line on the west, Rosecrans Avenue on the south, Western Avenue on the east, and Manchester Avenue on the north. More exact descriptions will be given wide publicity in the areas affected.

The Attorney General tomorrow will designate 27 other prohibited areas which the War Department has recommended; and additional areas a few days later.

†From: U.S., Congress, House, Tolan Committee, 77th Cong., 2d sess., 1942, H. Rept. 2124.

The final date after which no alien enemy may remain in or enter these two areas will be February 24. By that time all alien enemies in these areas will have their certificates of identification for which they must apply between February 2 and February 7, 1942.

The final date after which no alien enemy may remain in or enter these 27 areas will be February 15. Large numbers of alien enemies reside or are employed in prohibited areas Nos. 19 and 33 as distinguished from these 27 areas. It is, therefore, feasible to require removal and exclusion from these 27 areas at an earlier date.

The Department of Justice is being assisted in this program not only by the Departments of War and Navy, but also, among others, by the Departments of Labor and Treasury, the Farm Security Administration of the Department of Agriculture, the Federal Security Agency, the Work Projects Administration of the Federal Works Agency, and the Office of Facts and Figures.

In announcing the program, the Attorney General pointed out that the Federal Government which is in possession of all the facts is best equipped to take vigorous action in the interest of national security. He expressed his confidence that the program, requiring the coordination of all Federal and State agencies, will receive the cooperation of the entire public including the alien enemies involved. Their exclusion from the prohibited areas not only will aid national defense but also will protect the aliens themselves.

The Attorney General emphasized that, in the interests of an efficient and speedy solution of the problem, local officials and the public at large should leave this complicated program in the hands of the Federal Government and should not take conflicting action which might impede the program.

Thomas Clark who was appointed yesterday by the Attorney General as Coordinator of the Alien Enemy Control program for the Western Defense Command will be charged with execution of the plan.

Memo from Brigadier General Clark

Document 4†

GENERAL HEADQUARTERS, U.S. ARMY
Army War College
Washington, D.C.

January 26, 1942

MEMORANDUM FOR COMMANDING GENERAL OF THE FIELD FORCES:

Subject: Enemy Aliens on Pacific Coast.

1. You will recall that during my verbal report to you last Saturday, I included a statement with regards General DeWitt's concern over the large number of enemy aliens in his theater of operations.

2. You directed me to prepare a memorandum to the President on this subject.

3. I have discussed this matter with General Gullion and he has obtained from General DeWitt the latter's recommendations for restricting enemy aliens from certain areas on the West Coast. General Gullion concurs in General DeWitt's recommendations and has transmitted them by letter of January 25th (copy attached) to The Attorney General. I am told that The Secretary of War signed this letter yesterday. The Attorney General has full authority to take the action recommended by General DeWitt and concurred in by this headquarters.

4. I, therefore, recommend that you withhold sending a memorandum to the President until it is determined what action The Attorney General will take. Should his action not be all that is desired, then, in my opinion, would be the appropriate time to go to the President.

5. General Gullion is keeping closely in touch with this matter and will keep you advised if further action is necessary.

MARK W. CLARK,
Brigadier General, G.S.C.,
Deputy Chief of Staff.

†From: Record Group 407, National Archives, Washington, D.C.

5

The Problem in Hawaii

Document 5†

Date — July 3, 1942

MEMORANDUM FOR THE PRESIDENT:

Presidential approval was given on March 13th to a directive proposed by the Joint Chiefs of Staff which would authorize the Commanding General, Hawaiian Department, to evacuate to the mainland of the United States for internment in concentration camps Japanese residents of the Hawaiian Islands, either United States citizens or aliens, who were considered by appropriate authorities in the Islands to constitute a source of danger.

It has been found that this procedure is not feasible, as through application for a writ of habeus corpus any United States citizen can obtain release from custody. Consequently, agreement was reached by the Secretary of War and the Secretary of the Navy that family groups of Japanese ancestry should be evacuated to the mainland for resettlement, rather than internment. Tentative arrangements have been made with the War Relocation Authority for the resettlement of up to fifteen thousand persons.

We now wish to recommend that the directive approved on March 13th, 1942, be rescinded, and that the following be substituted therefor:

"No United States citizen of any derivation whatsoever, either naturalized or native-born, now residing in Hawaii, and considered by appropriate authority in the Hawaiian Islands to constitute a source of danger to our national security, will be transferred to the continental United States for internment. Such individuals will be interned in the Hawaiian Islands under authority vested in the Military Governor. Further, the Commanding General, Hawaiian Department, is authorized to evacuate to the United States, for resettlement in areas to be established by the War Relocation Authority, up to fifteen thousand persons, in family groups, from among the United States citizens of Japanese ancestry who may be considered as potentially dangerous to national security."

Approval of the foregoing by the President is respectfully requested.

E.J. KING
Commander in Chief, U.S. Fleet

G.C. MARSHALL
Chief of Staff

---

†From: President's Secretary's File, Franklin D. Roosevelt Library, Hyde Park, New York.

6

Debates and Plans in the Government

Document 6†

Transcript of Telephone Conversation

Jan. 29, 1942

Bendetson: This is Bendetson. How are you?

Mr. Rowe: I'm unhappy on account of prohibited areas and things.

B: I guess the Army certainly gives headache powders, the wrong kind though.

R: I think so.

B: Well, I have another one. As a matter of fact, I think you already have the word on this but I'm not sure. At any rate, it concerns Bainbridge Island in Puget Sound. Apparently Admiral Freeman . . .

R: Oh, that's the one that was sent to Ennis. And he sent it to you.

B: Is that the way it was?

R: He said that he had been working on what might be a false assumption, the Army was going to clear the stuff with the Navy.

B: Well, no, that's correct. They have cleared with it. But this relates to more, the request is that it be declared a restricted area to all concerned.

R: You mean prohibited or restricted?

B: I'm using your terms, prohibited to all concerned including citizens, except that those who are not of Japanese extraction can be permitted. Can you do that?

R: I don't know.

B: Can you keep citizens out?

R: We haven't got any jurisdiction. Maybe the Navy has. Maybe you guys can put your guards out and say get the hell out. Are there people living on it?

B: There are people living on it, yes. It's quite a large island.

R: What's so important about it?

B: Well, apparently there are several things important about it. One, shipbuilding. Two, aircraft warning service.

†From: Record Group 389, National Archives, Washington, D.C.

R: If there's aircraft warning service, the Army can just keep people out themselves, can't they?

B: Well, I think so, perhaps they could.

R: The Department just can't tell citizens to get off. —— if you can do it as a military problem some way.

B: Of course there are a number of citizens on there whom they want to remain, naturally, those employed in ship building.

R: They just want the Jap citizens off.

B: That's right. All enemy aliens and all people of Japanese extraction.

R: Has this been cleared through General DeWitt?

B: Yes.

R: And when do they want that done? Tomorrow, I suppose.

B: As soon as possible, Jim. That awful headache; I'm sorry to give you so many, Jim.

R: Well, I'll talk to Ed about it. I don't know how they can just kick a lot of citizens out in a prohibited area because if you do that then every area you've already requested, you'll want citizens kicked out too, American citizens of Japanese extraction.

B: That might come, yes. Of course it's not before us now but it might come.

R: Oh, well, if we do it once, we'll have it the next day. The Navy will say Terminal Island.

B: Well, Terminal Island of course is not in this yet. They want to treat that specially. Both Admiral Holmes and Admiral Greenslade and General DeWitt have talked about that a good deal, and they really do want to clear everybody off of that, but they might buy it.

R: The only thing that bothers me, if we agree on one we might as well admit that we're going to have the problem in every prohibited area, they'll want all Jap citizens out. But anyway I don't know that we can do it. I'll talk to Mr. Ennis and see what his thoughts are, and we'll talk to you this afternoon.

B: All right, Jim, fine. I'll stand by and be available on it. Thank you.

Document 6-a†

Transcript of Telephone Conversation

1/29/42
12:25 P.M.

Bendetsen: Hello, General DeWitt, how are you, Sir?

DeWitt: Just fine.

B: I got a call from Justice Department, Mr. Rowe called, in connection with the proposed restricted area on Bainbridge Island. He states that they have gotten a call from the Navy Department which indicates that they would prefer that it be classed as an area on which all would be excluded. That is, irrespective of whether they are Japanese of the first generation or Japanese aliens.

D: In other words, everybody.

B: Yes, sir. All people.

D: I would prefer that too and I am certain the Navy would.

. . . .

B: All people of Japanese extraction, that would include Japanese Americans and Japanese aliens.

D: That is exactly right.

D: What I told Admiral Freeman [was] that I was in complete agreement and to ask him whether or not he felt it was necessary for me to combine with him in presenting that matter to the War Department. Now, they did not feel it was necessary, but I was going to do it anyhow in the form of a radio, referring to Admiral Freeman's request to Chief of Naval Operations and state that I concurred in his request, that we were in agreement. Will that be sufficient?

B: Yes, sir. I am sure that it will, and I will so advise them informally.

D: —— a little further than that, is that right?

B: Well, that apparently is the idea. Yes, sir.

D: Well, I will call up Admiral Freeman—and find out—and tell him about your message, our telephone conversation, and ask him if he will agree to that. I am certain he will, but I think as a matter of fact, Bendetsen, if they get those of Japanese extraction off the Island, they get everybody off.

B: I see, of course there are a number of summer homes on Bainbridge Island belonging to white residents and the question, of course, would arise whether there would be a desire to exclude these people.

D: Well, I think it is not his desire to do that. I will call up though and call you back as soon as I can get him.

B: All right, sir thank you very much

†From: Record Group 389, National Archives, Washington, D.C.

D: It will take me a little while—probably an hour and a half.

B: All right, sir, that will be soon enough, General. Thank you very much.

D: Tell the Justice Department that both the Army and Navy are in accord on that.

B: Yes, sir, I shall in the meanwhile tell them that as far as people of Japanese extraction are concerned that the Army and Navy are in accord.

D: Yes, and I have to verify the other.

B: Thank you, General, goodbye.

Document 6-b†

Transcript of Telephone Conversation

1/29/42

Between 12:00 and 1:00 P.M.

General DeWitt: I got Admiral Freeman on the phone. He says that he would like all enemy aliens and all people of Japanese extraction removed from the Island.

Major Bendetsen: All enemy aliens—

General DeWitt: All, because it is a very large Island and a great many people live there and there is a shipbuilding plant there. So, it is just the enemy aliens that he wants moved out including all of Japanese extraction, whether enemy aliens or not.

Major Bendetsen: Very well, Sir. Then the others, of course, I suppose in order to—if it were necessary to do this—in order to give it some satisfactory legal basis as far as the Justice Department is concerned why the others could be given permits, I suppose.

General DeWitt: You mean the American citizens?

Major Bendetsen: Oh yes Sir.

General DeWitt: I don't think it would be necessary to do that.

Major Bendetsen: It wouldn't.

General DeWitt: All Germans—referring only to non-Americans.

Major Bendetsen: Yes Sir. Enemy aliens of all classes.

General DeWitt: But in addition to that—

Major Bendetsen: All people of Japanese extraction. Yes Sir, I understand, that was certainly quick work General.

General DeWitt: (laughter) Oh yes, I can get 'em pretty quick you see.

Major Bendetsen: Yes Sir, I will call them right away.

General DeWitt: I will send a radio indicating my concurrence with the Admiral on it.

Major Bendetsen: Very well sir, fine. Thank you General. Goodbye.

†From: Record Group 389, National Archives, Washington, D.C.

Document 6-c†

Transcript of Telephone Conversation

1/30/42

General DeWitt: I just wanted to call up Bendetsen and tell him in connection with the data the Department of Justice wanted on Bainbridge Island proposition, I am getting that but it will be two or three days before I will have it down here and can send it in.

General Gullion: All right. Bendetsen is attending a conference on the hill with the Congressmen from California, I think also the Senator and Mr. Rowe and Mr. Ennis of the Department of Justice. I understand that those Congressmen are strongly urging the Department of Justice to hurry up that evacuation.

D: Fine. I hope they'll do it.

G: I regretted the publicity this morning. It was my understanding that Justice tried to give the newspapers the description of those areas but the papers did not print it. I don't see why they had to put it out anyhow.

D: I don't either but the papers out here gave the boundaries.

G: Good! Well, they didn't here. That's not so bad if they gave the boundaries out there.

D: No, and the reaction so far has been good. As far as I know, the publicity given to it was really of a pretty high order. The public opinion is very rapidly crystallizing out here on that subject.

G: How far west, but you probably don't want to talk about how far you are going to move those people.

D: No, but you know there is one group and a large group want to move them entirely out of the state, another group wants to move them to the middle west, and some of them want them to be left in California.

G: A resettlement proposition is quite a proposition.

D: It is a problem but it can be worked out. Some of them not less than 300 miles from the coast, but there's no difference of opinion about wanting them to go, and it can be done. I'm going to have a conference with the Governor and Mr. Clark on Monday at Sacramento. Mr. Clark has been designated by the Department of Justice as the liaison officer for Mr. Rowe with the Western Defense Command. I'm going to have a conference with him and Governor Olson at Sacramento, Monday morning at eleven o'clock, and apparently that is what they are going to talk about

†From: Record Group 389, National Archives, Washington, D.C.

more than anything else. The Governor is all for it and so is the Attorney General of California, Mr. Warner. [Earl Warren]

G: Then the only thing is to determine where they are going to be put. I gues you can help provide the guards to get them there.

General DeWitt: Yes. I am perfectly willing to undertake it provided, as I told Bendetsen, all the other government agencies concerned with it like the Immigration Service and probably the Department of Commerce or Agriculture and the F.B.I. . . . .

General Gullion: Are subject to your requisition?

D: Yes.

G: Well, we told the Chief of Staff that this morning.

7

Recommendations from the Congress

Document 7†

CONGRESS OF THE UNITED STATES
House of Representatives
Washington, D.C.

January 30, 1942.

Honorable Henry L. Stimson
The Secretary of War
Washington, D.C.

Dear Mr. Secretary:

Today representatives of the three Pacific Coast States held a meeting to consider the Pacific Coast Defense situation with reference to enemy aliens.

After discussing the question at length in conjunction with representatives of the War and Justice Departments the meeting adopted recommendations, copy of which I herewith enclose.

Trusting appropriate consideration may be given to these recommendations, I am

Sincerely yours,
[CLARENCE LEA]
Chairman
Of The Meeting.

I. Recommendation to President that War Department be given immediate and complete control over all alien enemies, as well as United States citizens holding dual citizenship in any enemy country, with full power and authority to require and direct the cooperation and assistance of all other agencies of government in exercising such control and in effectuating evacuation, resettlement, or internment.

II. Recommendation to the War Department and other interested agencies that the following program be initiated at once.

1. Designation by War Department of critical areas throughout the country and territorial possessions.

2. Immediate evacuation from critical areas of all enemy aliens and their families, including children under 21, whether aliens or not.

†From: Record Group 107, National Archives, Washington, D.C.

3. Temporary internment of evacuated aliens and families in available CCC camps pending completion of long-range resettlement or internment program.
4. Opportunity and federal assistance to *dual* citizens living in critical areas for voluntary resettlement as patriotic contribution.
5. Federal assistance to all uninterned alien enemies and *dual* citizens whose means of livelihood are affected either by execution of program outlined or by unemployment brought about by other factors.
6. Development and consummation as soon as possible of complete evacuation and resettlement or internment program covering all alien enemies and *dual* citizens wherever located.

8

Conversations Among the Military

Document 8†

Transcript of Telephone Conversation

1/30/42

Major Bendetsen: Hello, General DeWitt, how are you sir? I just came from Capitol Hill where I attended a meeting of the California delegation of Congress. There were two or three from Washington State as well. Mr. Rowe of the Attorney General's office and Edward J. Ennis, the chief of the alien control unit of the Justice Department, were also there. They went over the whole situation as they see it and asked Mr. Rowe for a report of his views. At the end of the meeting they adopted a suggested program, which they will also present on Monday to a joint meeting which they're supposed to have with their senators. I thought perhaps I should read just what they have in mind to you, and you could perhaps have it down on your recording machine.

General DeWitt: All right, it's being recorded now.

B: [Reads Congressional delegation statement.]

They were quite emphatic in their views. They seemed to be pretty well stirred up. They asked me to state what the position of the War Department was. I stated that I could not speak for the War Department, had not been authorized up on The Hill to do so. They asked me for my own views and I stated that the position of the War Department was this: that we did not seek control of the program, that we preferred it be handled by the civil agencies. However, the War Department would be entirely willing, I believed, perhaps upon consideration to accept the responsibility provided they accorded the War Department, and the Secretary of War, and the military commander under him, full authority to require the services of any other federal agency, and provided that

†From: Record Group 389, National Archives, Washington, D.C.

General DeWitt: federal agency was required to respond. That was the sum and substance of the meeting, General.

General DeWitt: That's good.

. . . .

I'm glad to see that action is being taken, I mean that somebody in authority begins to see the problem. . . .

Bendetsen: It's a serious problem, and I can appreciate that now public sentiment is beginning to become irresistible, and I think anything you recommend would certainly be backed up, as you have said already, strongly by the public.

DeWitt: It's crystallizing very rapidly out here. As I remember there is some division, something you read that would indicate something about dual citizens. If you're going to predicate anything on dual citizenship you're never going to be able to prove dual citizenship because under the Japanese law, if a child is born out here he's registered fourteen days after birth with the local consular agent. He became a Japanese citizen, but all the records were destroyed when war was declared.

B: Of course it would be impossible to prove. As I see it, I believe the thinking on these prohibited areas, in order to reach what they term dual citizens, I think it's got to come to this, that out of military necessity some of these areas would be prohibited to everybody concerned, whether they are citizens, white or Jap or black or brown, it doesn't matter, everybody is barred and can only enter on a pass or permit; that is, without any arbitrary classification. Say, for example, Bainbridge Island. Suppose it were designated as a prohibited area, prohibited to all except on pass or permit, just like a military reservation. I think it's going to come to that.

D: Yes. You see, now that these restricted areas are coming out, like the two that were announced yesterday, the papers out here . . . The question of patriotic compliance doesn't hold water. I think there's a little politics in that maybe. They ought to cut that thing out. There are going to be a lot of Japs who are going to say, "Oh, yes, we want to go, we're good Americans and we want to do everything you say", but those are the fellows I suspect the most.

Major Bendetsen: Definitely. The ones who are giving you only lip service are the ones always to be suspected.

General DeWitt: That's the idea. I'm going to read that thing over carefully and talk to you again tomorrow about it.

B: Thank you.

Document 8-a†

Transcript of Telephone Conversation

1/31/42

D: Bendetsen, I have taken that program you read to me over the telephone yesterday, that is, that program drafted by that committee of congressmen from California, and broken it down and under each paragraph indicated my comments. I want to read it to you, have you any way of recording it?

B: Yes, sir, the recorder is on.

D: . . . I do not feel that the War Department should be charged with resettlement. That should be handled by some civil agency of the government, but if it should be determined that all enemy aliens are to be evacuated from the Pacific Coast, the War Department can handle the evacuation to the point or points where the resettlement projects have been established. Or, if they are to be interned, the War Department can handle internment camps. If it is shown that the civil agencies now set up under the President's proclamations for this implementation cannot efficiently and effectively perform their duties, then the War Department will necessarily have to take over such implementation. As a matter of fact, the steps now being taken by the Attorney General through the Federal Bureau of Investigation will do nothing more than exercise a controlling influence and preventative action against sabotage. It will not, in my opinion, be able to stop it. The only positive answer to that question is evacuation of all enemy aliens on the West Coast, and their resettlement or internment and the positive control military or otherwise. Now with reference to the second paragraph—

B: May I ask you, sir, as to the first paragraph—On alien enemies in the last sentence . . . do you include Japanese Americans?

D: I include all Germans, all Italians who are alien enemies and all Japanese who are Native-born or foreign-born.

Major Bendetsen: All Japanese, irrespective of citizenship.

General DeWitt: That's it.

. . . .

Major Bendetsen: That's very sound, sir. They had the impression yesterday, I believe, that dual citizens as such included all Japanese citizens; that is, all American citizens of Japanese

---

†From: Record Group 389, National Archives, Washington, D.C.

extraction. I assume in your last comment that you mean to include all alien enemies in addition, all American citizens of Japanese extraction.

D: That's right.

B: And all Italian dual citizens. Is that what you mean, sir?

D: Yes.

B: Would you include all Italian dual citizens in that?

D: I think so. Now, did I place the following of priority from the standpoint of danger of these three groups? First, the Japanese, all prices [sic].

B: That is, all Japanese including aliens and American citizens of Japanese extraction in Class 1.

D: Yes. As the most dangerous. The next group, the Germans.

B: Second, the Germans. Yes, sir.

General DeWitt: The third group, the Italians.

Major Bendetsen: Yes, sir. Now to what extent do we have your permission to use that?

D: You can use it in any way you want to, at your own discretion.

B: [Raises question of a phased evacuation.]

D: No. I think they all ought to go at once.

B: I think so, too, sir. I don't think they should have an opportunity of notice to do their worst while they are waiting.

D: I'll tell you, Bendetsen, they won't get out till the 24th now.

B: Yes, sir, that's too long as it is.

D: Too long as it is and I've given personal instructions to troops, and have written to the governors and the commanding officers of all exempted stations in the theatre of operations to be on their guard completely during that period.

B: Very good. Very good, sir.

D: Because I think it's going to be a dangerous period.

Major Bendetsen: Oh yes, sir.

General DeWitt: I wouldn't agree with that. Don't pass it. We've waited too long as it is. Get them all out.

B: All at once. Well that really takes care of all three questions for me, then, sir.

D: All right, old man.

B: All right, sir. Thank you very much, General.

D: Not at all, Bendetsen, Good-bye.

B: We will keep you advised. Good-bye, sir.

Document 8-b†

Transcript of Telephone Conversation

1 Feb 42

General Gullion: General, Bendetsen is here, I want to talk to you first. He is listening to me. Are you recording that thing? Are you able to record this General?

General DeWitt: Yes, it is being recorded.

General Gullion: I have just returned from a conference in the Attorney General's Office. There were present Mr. Edgar Hoover, Mr. Rowe, Mr. McCloy, our Assistant Secretary of War, Mr. Ennis, the counsel for the Immigration Department of the Department of Justice—he is also Chief of the Enemy Aliens Control Division, Major Bendetsen and I; and Mr. Biddle was there.

They handed us a press release which they wanted the War Department to sponsor with The Department of Justice. I am going to read it to you, and we did not agree to it; we wanted to refer it to you and find out what you felt about it, and we also thought you might want to wait until after your conference at 11 at Sacramento tomorrow with the Governor and Mr. Clark before you let us know about it. Mr. Clark has been furnished a copy of this press release. Shall I read it to you.

General DeWitt: Yes please.

General Gullion: [Reads proposed press release.]

General Gullion: The government is fully aware of the problem presented by dual nationalities, particularly among the Japanese. Appropriate governmental agencies are now dealing with the problem. (Now watch this sentence—that is interjected by me). The Department of War and the Department of Justice are in agreement that the present military situation does not at this time require the removal of American citizens of the Japanese race.

I wouldn't agree to that.

General Gullion: I know that—final paragraph.

. . . .

General DeWitt: Yes, what I'll do after I get hold of the record, I'll read it over carefully and analyze from my viewpoint and then give you my comment. Now, I can say this right now as a result of the development of this situation out here as affected by the publication of these restricted areas out here; that is a means of control of the possible sabotage of enemy aliens, but it is not a positive . . .

†From: Record Group 389, National Archives, Washington, D.C.

It only can be made positive by removing those people who are aliens and who are Japs of American citizenship, away from the area. Until they are moved, we have no positive assurance irrespective of the—that sabotage will not occur because they are still present to accomplish it.

General Gullion: Now I might suggest General, Mr. McCloy was in the conference and he will probably be in any subsequent conference until we decide about this press release, and he has not had the benefit of all the conversations we have had with you—if you could give us something, not only in conversation, but a written thing that we could record, as stating your position, your recommendations and the reasons for your recommendations, that is, they want to know and McCloy also, we weren't able to tell the conference on what you based your recommendations, other than the reasons I suggested, that you had been on the job going up and down and that is what you had concluded.

General DeWitt: Yes, I will be glad to do that.

General Gullion: Now Bendetsen is here Sir. He may have some other points.

Major Bendetsen: Yes Sir, General DeWitt. I have nothing further to add in a general way. There are a few things that arose that it might be well to have recorded for your consideration in addition. As far as any action is concerned looking toward evacuation of persons involving citizens of the United States of Japanese extraction, they will have nothing apparently whatever to do with it. They say that if that comes to pass, if we recommend and it is determined that there should be a movement or evacuation of citizens, they say hands off, that it is the Army's job; that is point one that came up. Point two, they agree with us that it is possible from their standpoint, from a legal standpoint they say "yes" we can designate certain areas which are absolutely prohibited to all except those whom we permit to come in; in other words, the licensing theory that because of military necessity we say this is a prohibited area to all persons, irrespective of nationality and citizenship, and only those whom we license can come in or remain in. They agree with us that this could be done as the legal basis for exclusion, however, we insist that we could also say that while all whites could remain, Japs can't, if we think there is military necessity for that. They apparently want us to join with them so that if anything happens they would be able to say "this was the military recommendation."

General DeWitt: What they are trying to do, it looks to me just off the bat, without thinking it over, they are trying to cover themselves and lull the populace in to a false sense of security.

Major Bendetsen: Well, of course, the immediate occasion for the release is, that they know here that there is a very heavy sentiment on the West Coast for a Japanese evacuation but that is the immediate occasion for it—Biddle wants to as you say, have the people mollified on it, by being able to put forth the statement that in view of the military situation that there is no occasion for it. Well that of course is to protect themselves.

General DeWitt: Well I will read that thing over very carefully, I won't be able to get any answer to it until sometime Tuesday.
....

Major Bendetsen: All right Sir. Sometime Tuesday morning. Rowe also wanted to know just what the details would be if the Army were to undertake a mass evacuation.

General DeWitt: I tell you Bendetsen, I haven't gone into the details of it, but Hell, it would be no job as far as the evacuation was concerned to move 100,000 people.

Major Bendetsen: Put them on trains and move them to specified points.

General DeWitt: We could do it in job lots you see. We could take 4000 or 5000 a day, or something like that.

Major Bendetsen: We would have to put them in shelter that we could find inland—3 C camps inland, or National Guard areas under tentage inland, etc.

General DeWitt: With the men first.

Major Bendetsen: We are now making a survey here of all available shelter facilities to find out what there is that is not required for troops and we have asked the Corps Area Commanders to tell us about Fair Grounds and agricultural farms owned by the States, etc. I think we can find places for them.

General DeWitt: Yes, you see we would move the men first, then move the women and children after.

Major Bendetsen: Of course, there is a large administrative problem involved in keeping the record straight so that we would not have another Evangeline situation.

General DeWitt: Oh yes, we could work this up but I mean to say that it is an impossible task, or an extremely difficult task, I don't think so.

Major Bendetsen: No Sir, I agree. All right sir, we expect to have your comments sometime Tuesday morning after you have had the conference with Mr. Clark.

General DeWitt: You see I can't give the whole day to it, we are busy, but I will get after it Tuesday morning and hope to be able to telephone it to you sometime Tuesday afternoon but it may not be until Wednesday.

Major Bendetsen: All right Sir, we will keep you advised. Goodbye.

Document 8-c†

Transcript of Telephone Conversation

General Gullion
General Clark
Feb. 4, 1942.

General Clark: I've got to go to represent General Marshall up at a Congressional meeting this morning on—from Western Congressmen.

General Gullion: We've had a man up there, darn it, they are nothing but just a lot of bull.

Gen. Clark: Well, anyway I've been directed by General Marshall to get up there, and I presume, I anticipate some questions on this enemy alien thing. I wondered if you could bring me up to date just generally on that situation.

Gen. Gullion: Sunday afternoon, [Feb. 1] I was in a conference with Mr. McCloy and Bendetsen of my office, Mr. Biddle, Edgar Hoover, Mr. Rowe (you know who Rowe is), Rowe is the third man in the Department of Justice now; he was one of the President's anonymous six, the President put him over there and he ranks right after Fahy, the Solicitor, so if the Attorney General and Fahy were to go away, Rowe would be the Acting Attorney General, and Mr. Ennis, who is the head of their Emergency unit, and Solicitor also for the Immigration Bureau. Now here is the way the thing started. Mr. Rowe said well,—well that is immaterial what he said about Bendetsen, but then they said there is too much hysteria about this thing; said these Western Congressmen are just nuts about it and the people are getting hysterical and there is no evidence whatsoever of any reason for disturbing citizens, and the Department of Justice, Rowe started it and Biddle finished it—The Department of Justice will having nothing whatsoever to do with any interference with citizens, whether they are Japanese or not. They made me a little sore and I said, well listen Mr. Biddle, do you mean to tell me that if the Army, the men on the ground, determine it is a military necessity to move citizens, Jap citizens, that you won't

†From: Record Group 389, National Archives, Washington, D.C.

help us. He didn't give a direct answer, he said the Department of Justice would be through if we interfered with citizens and writs of habeas corpus, etc. Well, anyhow, then they presented to us a press release which they wanted us to sign up and put out on Sunday night. We agreed to everything at once in the press release except this sentence "The Department of War and the Department of Justice by an agreement that the present military situation does not at this time require the removal of American citizens of the Japanese race." Well, DeWitt had been telling us that he did not want to get all Japs out you know, of certain areas, and DeWitt had gone further than, he has withdrawn from that now partly, but in his talks with us he indicated pretty strongly that he thought there would have to be a mass evacuation of 117,000 Japs, citizens and aliens, out of California. Of course that would be a tremendous problem but it might have to be done. So, we would not agree with them on that; it wasn't any too pleasant a meeting and we agreed to call DeWitt up, read this press release to him and see what he was going to do. I sent you yesterday a ten page conversation with DeWitt. I don't know whether it has reached you or not.

Gen. Clark: No Sir, I have not seen it.

General Gullion: Ask Miss so and so—Miss Noble what she did, she said she was sending it to Gen. Clark, GHQ. We called DeWitt up Sunday night and read this press release to him, he said he was going to have a meeting at 11 o'clock Monday morning at Sacramento with the Governor and with Mr. Clark, representative of the Department of Justice on the West Coast, and that he would give us his views on the press release and his recommendations after he came back from that meeting. Well, he wasn't able to do it because the meeting lasted long and the thing I read him over the phone was garbled in the recording and he couldn't tell much about it so he had us read another copy to him, and so at noon yesterday, 1:30 yesterday Secretary Stimson, McCloy, Bendetson and I talked for an hour and a half on the situation and I can tell you that the two Secretaries are against any mass movement. They are pretty much against it. And they are also pretty much against interfering with citizens unless it can be done legally. Well, I think McCloy did say this to Biddle—you are putting a wall street lawyer in a helluva box, but if it is a question of the safety of the country [and] the constitution . . . why the constitution is just a scrap of paper to me. That is what McCloy said. But they are just a little afraid DeWitt hasn't enough grounds to justify any movements of that kind.

General Clark: Well, what do you think should be done? What is the position of the War Department?

General Gullion: Well, the War Department's position is of course what Stimson's and McCloy's position is, that is all.

General Clark: In other words, not to move them but take out some aliens.

General Gullion: Well, we have agreed this far, everybody has agreed this far. DeWitt has sent these maps of California and yesterday Washington and Oregon arrived so we have them all now, part of Arizona too. Now, he has agreed and the Department of Justice has agreed and the Secretary of War has agreed that they will move out of certain restricted areas all aliens. Now that doesn't touch citizens at all and personally I don't think that is going to cure the situation much.

General Clark: All enemy aliens.

General Gullion: If anything, I think it is a provocative move.

General Clark: How many does that involve in California?

General Gullion: It is estimated between 7 and 11,000.

General Clark: How many in the other States. . .?

General Gullion: I don't know because that thing didn't get here until yesterday. Let me get Bendetsen on that, I haven't seen the papers.

General Clark: That has already been published.

General Gullion: The California thing is.

General Clark: The Proclamation by the Department of Justice has gone out requiring that enemy aliens move out of certain areas. That was waterfront—

Gen. Gullion: Yes, the Embardadero and all that stuff.

General Clark: Now they are not going to try to take care of those citizens in the Government, they are just going to move them to other locations.

General Gullion: No there is nothing said about it—denying reentry to those places. Category A—is an absolute prohibition on reentry. Category B, that is other areas not so sensitive, they can reenter upon permission and that is what has been proposed—been suggested in our conference with the Department of Justice. Instead of moving out 117,000 Japanese, that a system of licensing, permission— everybody must move out except those you are permitted to stay, and that would get around the constitutional part of it; that is, we could deny white citizens the right to stay unless we gave them a permit to stay. Now, I didn't quite tell you what DeWitt read us yesterday. It was a 10 page thing he read us over the telephone to McCloy, and I had it recorded and had it typed and that is the thing I sent you a copy of. Have you had a chance to study that thing Bendetsen, (Yes Sir I have) well I wish you would tell him. I read it over hastily and sent it on down to McCloy and I haven't read it but once. I wish you would tell General Clark what he proposed.

Major Bendetsen: He states, in substance, General Clark, that the California State authorities believe that they can take action which would be designed to provide for the complete evacuation of alien enemies and voluntarily of Japanese citizens of the United States, to other areas in California not close to what are termed critical areas. Of course, there has been no conference with the Governors of Oregon or Washington. It is only California, and that in turn is based on the fact that apparently California expects that the Federal Government will actually step in and finance it. That is, a resettlement project, is what it would be. However, that proceeds on the theory that you can get rid of all undesirables from certain critical areas by merely moving the alien enemies and then saying to the others, we ask that you move voluntarily. I don't think it will work and I don't think it should be done by the States in the first place. I think it should be a uniform plan under Federal control.

General Clark: Well, I've got that picture; in other words, the War Department as represented by the two Secretaries (General Gullion just told me) feels that there should not be any mass movement and rather feel that we should leave it the way it is, having denied them access to certain areas.

Maj. Bendetson: Well, I am not so sure Sir, that they feel that we should leave it as it is. For example, I think that they might entertain this. We have what are now called by the Justice Department, prohibited areas. Now I think the plan perhaps to which the Secretaries might agree to would be this. To have a third type of Area. Area type No. 1 might be called a military area, from which you would exclude all persons except those who had permits. Area 2 would be a prohibited area from which all alien enemies would be excluded. Area 3, would be a restricted area from which alien enemies would be excluded except on pass or permit. Those are the three types now in view. Now I think they might go for this: A combination of 1 and 3, that is to say, create Islands around your vital installations, declare those areas as type one.

General Clark: Nobody except by permit.

Major Bendetsen:	Then create a strip of type 3 along the coastal frontier say, just along the coastal frontier from which you would evacuate all aliens, except those who had permits. Now a combination of 1 and 3 I think might be acceptable from what they indicated yesterday. Don't you think so General Gullion?
Gen. Gullion:	Yes.
Maj. Bendetsen:	I have prepared a memorandum last night which is now being typed of that kind of plan.
General Clark:	Well, I just wanted to get the picture General Gullion, because going down there, this whole thing is the defense of the West Coast and I knew that this thing would come up and I just wanted to know generally what the latest set up was. You rather expect the Department of Justice to follow with Washington and Oregon and the other States with the same thing that they have already put out in California.
Gen. Gullion:	Oh that will come out.
Maj. Bendetsen:	They have the Oregon and Washington restricted areas in their hands now General Clark. They got them at 5 o'clock and I talked last night to the second assistant Attorney General and he said we could expect that they would take the same action on those.
General Clark:	And that just excludes all the alien enemies only.
Maj. Bendetsen:	Yes Sir. It doesn't reach the Japanese citizens.
General Clark:	Now, does that include Boeing Plant, do you recall?
Maj. Bendetsen:	Yes Sir, it includes all the area in Washington State from Sumas straight down to Vancouver lying to the West. In other words, it includes all of Puget Sound, all of the east shore of Puget Sound, the Olympic Penninsula, Gray's Harbor, Willapa the mouth of the Columbia and Portland.
General Clark:	You mean everybody has to get all enemy aliens out of that area.
Maj. Bendetsen:	Yes Sir, that is Category A. That includes of course all the Japanese around the Boeing Plant down there in the Kenton-Auburn District out of Seattle and all of them along the waterfronts in Takoma, Seattle, but it leaves the Nisei all around in there, all around Willapa Harbor and the mouth of the Columbia and Mikado and all that.
Gen. Clark:	That will probably involve quite a resettlement.
Maj. Bendetsen:	Well there are about 14,000 Japs, including Nisei in that area, of which about 3000 only are aliens.
General Gullion:	Now on that matter of statistics, I want to verify what I told General Clark. You know originally we were told that there were 7000 Japanese in the California area that would be affected.

Maj. Bendetsen: 7000 alien enemies in the California category A.

General Gullion: Well, now how does that figure go up. It was raised to more than 7000. Who else was included in that.

Maj. Bendetsen: Well, if you would include all the Nisei, plus all alien enemies for all the category A areas on the 3 coast states you would have closer to 30,000 people because in those areas are the bulk of the Japanese. There are 93,500 Japanese in California including Nisei.

General Clark: Now what is this Nisei?

Maj. Bendetsen: Yes Sir, the second generation and the third generation. They are the people who are citizens, and you have 14,500 in Washington State, around as I have said, 93,500 in California, including Nisei, and if you would remove all of those, that is the second generation Japanese who are citizens, plus all enemy aliens from all of the restricted areas designated by General DeWitt in his recommendations, you would get up around 30,000 people.

General Clark: Well thank you, General, I've gotten the big picture and I appreciate the time you have given me Sir.

General Gullion: All right. Glad to have talked to you.

CC: Col. Carrington
     Maj. Bendetsen
     Miss Wisch
     Miss Brocklemann

(Transcribed by Helen Noble, Feb. 4, 1942)

Document 8-d†

Transcript of Telephone Conversation

3 February 1942

Chief of Staff,
General George C. Marshall: Is there anything you want to say now about anything else? Of course we're on an open phone.

DeWitt: We're on an open phone, but George I can talk a little about this alien situation out here.

Marshall: Yes.

DeWitt: I had a conference yesterday with the Governor and several representatives from the Department of Justice and Department of Agriculture with a view to removal of the Japanese from where they are now living to other portions of the state.

†From: Record Group 107, National Archives, Washington, D.C.

Marshall: Yes.

DeWitt: And the Governor thinks it can be satisfactorily handled without having a resettlement somewhere in the central part of the United States and removing them entirely from the state of California. As you know the people out here are very much disturbed over these aliens, the Japanese being among them, and want to get them out of the several communities.

Marshall: Yes.

DeWitt: And I've agreed that if they can solve the problem by getting them out of the areas limited as the combat zone, that it would be satisfactory. That would take them about 100 to 150 miles from the coast, and they're going to do that I think. They're working on it.

Marshall: Thank you.

DeWitt: The Department of Justice has a representative out here, and the Department of Agriculture, and they think the plan is an excellent one. I'm only concerned with getting them away from around these aircraft factories and other places.

Marshall: Yes. Anything else?

DeWitt: No, that's all.

Marshall: Well, good luck.

Document 8-e†

Transcript of Telephone Conversation

Feb. 3, 1942
2:00 P.M.

Mr. McCloy: Feel concerned that the Army, that means you in that area, should not take the position even in your conversations with the political figures out there that it favors a wholesale withdrawal of all Japanese citizens and aliens from the Coast, for the reason that it may get us into a number of complications which we have yet not seen the end of. We have about reached the point where we feel that perhaps the best solution of it is to limit the withdrawal to certain prohibited areas. There are so many legal questions involved in discrimination between the native born Japanese (that is the American citizens) and the aliens, in the first place; and, in the second place, there are so many that would be involved in a mass withdrawal, the social and economic disturbances would be so great that we would like to go a little slowly on it, and we are a little afraid that if it gets about out there that the Army is really taking the position on mass withdrawal, that it may stimulate—

General DeWitt: Mr. Secretary, I have been trying to do that and I think I have succeeded, I haven't taken any position.

Mr. McCloy: Good, good.

General DeWitt: But I did prepare a memorandum for you that I was going to telephone to General Gullion as he had a recording machine there to tell you about that press release.

"MEMORANDUM for the Assistant Secretary.

I have carefully studied the transcript of the joint release by the Secretary of War and the Attorney General with respect to the control of alien enemies on the West Coast. A draft of same is attached hereto with proposed changes therein, suggested by the undersigned. So as to so work it and assure its accuracy and to make it to conform to prospective future action which may be necessary to make the control of alien enemies now initiated by the announcement of restricted areas more positive. The important changes made by the undersigned, other than in certain wording, has been to eliminate in the last sentence of paragraph 4, the words "these steps will insure compliance with the control of alien enemies exercised in the restricted area" and to eliminate the last sentence of paragraph 8 reading "The Department of War and the Department of

†From: Record Group 107, National Archives, Washington, D.C.

Justice are in agreement that the present military situation, does not at this time require the removal of American citizens of the Japanese Race"; and to change the last paragraph to read as follows:

"The Secretary of War, General DeWitt, The Attorney General and the director of the Federal Bureau of Investigation believe that the steps taken to date for the control of alien enemies has been appropriate and such additional steps to insure this control will be taken in the future as may be found necessary and advisable."

The reason for the changes in the proposed press release attached hereto and indicated above, are as follows: The undersigned attended a conference in the office of Governor Olsen of California at 11:00 P.M. yesterday, February 2nd, that six were present, Mr. Thomas G. Clark of the office of the Attorney General, Mr. C. Murray Thompson, Department of Agriculture, Mr. Wm. K. Cecil, Director of Agriculture of the State of California, Col. Donald A. Stroh, General Staff Corps, Assistant G-2, Western Defense Command in the 4th Army, and Col. J.F. Watson, Judge Advocate, Western Defense Command 4th Army, at which conference the question of control of alien enemies was discussed insofar as it affected the designation of restricted areas announced by the Attorney General, particularly as pertains to the Japanese population of the State now employed or living on agricultural land.

It was the concensus of opinion of all present that the registration of alien enemies of the Japanese race and the furnishing of each such alien an identification card, and the requirement that they carry such identification card on their person at all times, will not solve the problem or insure the denial of entrance to such restricted areas. By these steps alone, Japanese American citizens could not and would not be distinguished from alien enemy Japanese. That to protect the Japanese of American birth from suspicion and arrest, they should also have to carry identification cards to prove that they are not enemy aliens, as the enemy alien by not carrying identification card on his person could claim to be an American Japanese. In other words, all Japanese look alike and those charged with the enforcement of the regulation of excluding alien enemies from restricted areas will not be able to distinguish between them. The same applies in practically the same way to alien Germans and alien Italians but due to the large number of Japanese in the State of California (approximately 93,000), larger than any other State in the Union, and the very definite war consciousness of the people of California, as far as pertains to the Japanese participation in the war, the question of the alien Japanese and all Japanese presents a problem in control, separate and distinct from that of the German or Italian.

The general concensus of opinion as agreed to by all present at this conference was that, due to the above facts, the removal of all male adult Japanese, that is over 18 years of age, whether native or American born, alien enemy or Japanese, from that area of California defined as a combat zone——but before consideration be given to the question of their removal from the State of California and the inauguration or initiation of resettlement projects be made by the State authorities to determine whether or not suitable areas could be found in the State of California east of the line limiting the combat zone on which these people could be settled to produce the products which they are now producing in the defined restricted areas or in the vicinity thereof. It was suggested that the cost of movement and resettlement of these Japanese, if found feasible, be borne either by the Federal Government or that the assets of aliens and alien governments now in the United States be liquidated and used to finance the program.

. . . .

That the Governor of California would contact prominent leaders of the American born Japanese and ask them in their capacity as American citizens to adopt this movement as a logical and reasonable one on the basis that as loyal American citizens, such action was necessary in order to insure the security the West Coast of the United States. As a necessary protective measure for the Japanese themselves. As a means of continuing the type of employment to which they were particularly adapted, and assure no shortage of production of produce that is essential to the National Defense.

The undersigned agreed that if such a step was found to be reasonable, it would remove that element in the population most dangerous to proper measures for the defense of the Coast and protection of the vital installations therein. That the combat zone in which these vital installations were located would be freed of their presence and that an area east of the eastern limit of the combat zone would constitute a protective measure for the defense of the West Coast as far as California is concerned.

It was agreed that an effort should be made to solve the question of Japanese aliens in this way as it had good prospects of being carried out successfully. The meeting then adjourned.

The problem of the alien German and the alien Italian, while a difficult one, has not the same features as the Japanese problem and can be handled without consideration of their removal from the state or scattered areas within the state. It is going to be a difficult matter to assure that enemy aliens will not enter Category A restricted areas whatever their nationality. The only deterrent will be the fear of internment if caught in such an area.

The undersigned feel that it will also be found necessary to require all American citizens who may work or have businesses in such areas to carry identification cards for their protection, similar to the identification cards now prescribed by the War Department for all commissioned officers of the Army, and that frequent inspections by the proper authorities will have to be made of these areas to check against possible entry by aliens. For the above reasons I recommend that the proposed press release be changed as indicated because if this is not done, I feel that otherwise the release, as it is worded at present, will have a tendency to mollify or lull into a sense of false security the people of the state of California who are fully alive to the ever-present internal danger of having 260,000 enemy aliens in their midst, and the resulting increase in the external danger which is intensified by such a large number of aliens living in the area."

I have typewritten that and am going to mail it.

Mr. McCloy: Good.

Gen. DeWitt: The Governor (this is their suggestion; Mr. Clark and Mr. [Thompson] agreed), The Governor in looking at the map and going over the various agricultural areas, some of which are close to and are really superimposed on the restricted areas, that there were other areas adjacent to them and not far from them, about 100 to 150 miles from the coast, that these people could be moved to, and it wouldn't involve very many Japanese; that is to say, he thought the total amount in the whole state would be around 20,000.

Mr. McCloy: The total amount that would have to be moved?

Gen. DeWitt: Yes.

. . . .

Gen. DeWitt: By working through them to put it on a voluntary basis. That's what he wants to do, and he feels by working through these Japanese leaders he can.

Mr. McCloy: That he can do it. Well, that introduces a new element. But the bad ones won't volunteer, will they?

Gen. DeWitt: What's that?

Mr. McCloy: The bad ones, the ones that are foreign agents, that are sympathetic with Japan, will not volunteer, will they?

Gen. DeWitt: Mr. McCloy, we can move them anyhow. We have 30,000 of those people who are aliens, who are in the alien enemy class.

Mr. McCloy: Well, that's a different thing.

Gen. DeWitt: Yes. There are 30,000 but that's men, women, and children. When you take the male over 14, it'll cut that down quite materially, how much it's going to be we don't know yet; that's what they're figuring out now. His idea is that you don't have to worry about the alien enemy group. The other group, the American Jap, the civilians, the citizens, to move voluntarily under the leadership of these . . .

Mr. McCloy: Well, suppose he does not move?

Gen. DeWitt: Then I don't know how they're going to handle it. He thinks that can be done that way.

Mr. McCloy: I have no doubt that if the thing were properly organized there could be a big voluntary mass movement, but there would be bound to be cases, I should think, where some of them would not move, and in that case we would be up against the question as to whether we could move the American citizen of Japanese race. We have felt here that there are so many complications involved in a compulsory movement of any great size that would involve the [Nisei?] I think you call them, that is to say the Japanese Americans, that the best way to solve it, at least for the time being, would be to establish limited restricted zones around the airplane plants, the forts and the other important military installations, but do that merely on a military basis, and when you've done it on that basis, establish a system of licensing whereby you permit to come back into that area all non-suspected citizens. You may, by that process, eliminate all of the Japs, but you might conceivably permit some to come back whom you are quite certain are free from any suspicion, as well as the fact that you might let some Italians come back. Now that has sound legal basis for it.

Gen. DeWitt: Particularly about the Germans and the Italians because you don't have to worry about them as a group. You have to worry about them purely as certain individuals. Out here, Mr. Secretary, a Jap is a Jap to these people now.

Mr. McCloy: Yes, I can understand that.

Gen. DeWitt: The Governor said yesterday, I sat on the sidelines, the Governor said yesterday that if something isn't done and done very promptly, why in certain sections of the state they're going to take it into their own hands.

Mr. McCloy: Yes, that's what we fear.

. . . .

Gen. DeWitt: I'm going to dictate a redraft of press release. I read it to Mr. Clark from the Department of Justice, who agreed with it and he thinks it's been improved and made a little more accurate. I was now going to read it to Major Bendetsen or General Gullion over the phone and then mail it so it could be gotten to the press.

Mr. McCloy: Yes. Well, you don't need that now because it's been recorded.

Gen. DeWitt: Well I haven't read that—I don't know that I've read the press release—yes I did, I read it.

. . . .

Gen. DeWitt: There are some things I wanted to tell you about the Japanese. I think in view of the very energetic steps that are now being taken, that I just referred to, that nothing can be done until, nothing further rather, until they have thoroughly explored the prospects of doing that success- fully. It's the idea of the state authorities, and it's their idea only. If it can be done, it certainly is going to remove the pressure on the military. I'm furnishing just 23,000 guards from the troops that ought to be gotten back to training, and if that can be done, and they can be moved successfully to land, productive land, from that area, it is going to be extremely helpful to me and I'm perfectly willing to accept it as a measure of protection, but if they are allowed to remain where they are, we are just going to have one complication after another, because you just can't tell one Jap from another. They all look the same. Give a sentry or an officer or troops any job like that, a Jap's a Jap, and you can't blame the man for stopping all of them.

. . . .

Mr. McCloy: Yes. Now let me get one more thought clear. If these fellows do not proceed apace with this new suggestion of theirs, I wonder whether it wouldn't be practicable to put into effect a withdrawal from these limited restricted zones, a withdrawal which would include not only Japanese aliens but also Japanese citizens on the basis of excluding from a military reservation any one that you wanted to.

Gen. DeWitt: Since the announcement of the restricted areas, those aliens now in them are beginning to move out.

Mr. McCloy: Those are the aliens but I am talking to you about the citizens as well, the Japanese American citizens.

Gen. DeWitt: They are not touched by this you see.

Mr. McCloy: They wouldn't be touched by what is going on now?
Gen. DeWitt: No.
Mr. McCloy: As I understand it, you are only removing the aliens from those restricted areas.
Gen. DeWitt: That is all, that is all under the restricted areas as designated by the Attorney General is applicable only to enemy aliens.
Mr. McCloy: That is right. Now, my suggestion is that (after we have talked it over with General Gullion and Major Bendetsen) we might call those military reservations in substance, and exclude everyone—whites, yellows, blacks, greens—from that area and then license back into the area those whom we felt there was no danger to be expected from.
Gen. DeWitt: Oh I see.
Mr. McCloy: You see, then we cover ourselves with the legal situation is taken care of in that way because in spite of the constitution you can eliminate from any military reservation, or any place that is declared to be in substance a military reservation, anyone—any American citizen, and we could exclude everyone and then by a system of permits and licenses permitting those to come back into that area who were necessary to enable that area to function as a living community. Everyone but the Japs—
    . . . .
Mr. McCloy: It would be a big administrative job but I think you might cut corners, you might announce the same day that you declare it to be a reservation, you announce it the same moment that everyone is excluded from it but everybody in this category can come in, and in due course they will get a permit as soon as they can get around to it, giving them the right to come in. In the meantime the Japs would have to be out of there, or any other dangerous alien, and now we would eliminate in that way anybody that we wanted to. Now, you can do that on a military reservation without suspending writs of Habeas Corpus and without getting into very important legal complications, and that is a consideration that you might bear in mind. . . . You couldn't do it on a very large scale but you could do it on a substantial scale around we will say the Boeing Plant, the Consoliated Plant or some of your ports or your harbor installations. . . .

Document 8-f†

Transcript of Telephone Conversation

Feb. 4, 1942

General Gullion: Hello.

General DeWitt: Hello, who is this?

General Gullion: This is Gullion. We just had a long conference this afternoon with Mr. Rowe, Mr. Ennis, Mr. [?] of the Justice Department. Bendetsen and I did before Mr. McCloy. He was present. And they, as Bendetsen told you, were resisting the publication of these Washington areas because they want some explanation of it; and then we adjourned for a moment to telephone that to you, and then the main reason they came over there was to get us to get that press release out. They would not accept it as amended by you, and inasmuch as when I read it the other day it didn't take very well, I am going to have Bendetsen read it to you, the pertinent paragraph—just one paragraph, the final paragraph, and we want to know what you thought about it. He will read it to you.

Col. Bendetsen: Oh yes Sir, General.

General DeWitt: Hello Colonel, how are you. I just heard about it. [Bendetsen's promotion]

Col. Bendetsen: Thank you, I just did too. All right Sir, here it is, "The Attorney General and the Director of the Federal Bureau of Investigation believe that the steps taken todate for the control of alien enemies have been appropriate. The Secretary of War and General DeWitt state that the Attorney General has taken all steps recommended by the War Department for control of alien enemies in the West Coast States to date." That is in lieu of the concluding paragraph as previously submitted.

General DeWitt: Now, as I have just heard it once, as I see that it would appear as if the Department of Justice would like to get out this release to indicate that they have done everything that the War Department has asked and the War Department is satisfied with what they have done so far. Now, but it seems to me that it has back of it the thought that if the War Department recommends anything additional why there may be some—in other words, it is laying the ground for a possible disagreement and the Attorney General not doing any more.

†From: Record Group 389, National Archives, Washington, D.C.

Col. Bendetsen: That is right Sir, it lays the ground work for exactly that. That is what I am afraid of. I think they have in mind today, and Rowe so expressed himself on several occasions that they want to step out of this picture.

. . . .

Col. Bendetsen: It doesn't mean that, as far as a public statement is concerned it doesn't suggest that but it does suggest that they have in mind the fact that they may balk to us. The implication to us on the inside is just as you point out, and I think from what Rowe said today on repeated occasions that they are laying the foundation for an exit, and I don't think we can stop that. In other words, General DeWitt when we come to the point of excluding Japanese citizens which I am sure we are going to have to do, from some areas at least, that is American citizens of Japanese extraction, I am sure we are going to have to do that aren't we. Well now, when we come to that, they are not going to go along with us.

General DeWitt: Well now in connection with that for a minute. I have just talked to Mr. Thompson from the Department of Agriculture and Mr. Clark from the Department of Justice, I mean from the Attorney General's office. They came in to see me for a few minutes—I said I had just talked to you before noon, before 10:30, about that time, and they said in working up the data that Governor Olsen had asked them to work up to determine whether or not they were agricultural areas outside the combat zone that they could move these people to, all Japanese the Governor is for moving along and says the people are pushing him to do it, whether they are American citizens or not, to move agricultural areas away from the coast.

. . . .

Col. Bendetsen: That would just about be the eastern half of the Sacramento, San Joaquin, and the Imperial Valley.

General DeWitt: Well, I told them it looked good to me but I wanted to see the exact location of each area on the map and that in principal I agreed to it, and I think that is the way it is going to come out, and if it does I think it will be satisfactory from a defense standpoint as well as from an agricultural standpoint. Mr. Clark immediately spoke up and said well if you will agree to that General, our problems are over.

. . . .

General DeWitt: You see the situation is this. I have never on my own initiative, recommended a mass evacuation, or the removal of any Jap other than an alien. In other words, I have made no distinction between an alien—whether he is Jap, Italian or German, that they must all get out of the Category A area.

Col. Bendetsen: Yes Sir, the prohibited areas.

General DeWitt: The agitation to remove all Japanese away from the Coast, and some suggested out of California entirely, is within the State, the population of the State which has been espoused by the Governor. I have never been a party to that but I have said "if you do that, and can solve that problem, it will be a positive step towards the protection of the coast."

Col. Bendetsen: Definitely so, of course.

. . . .

General DeWitt: I told Mr. Clark and Mr. Thompson this morning, I won't commit myself to agreeing to that change in plan until I have studied the map, until I have an opportunity to look at the areas on the map that they suggested to move all those Japs to. I told them this, "If you—what you suggest can be done, I will assist you in every way by giving my consent to it, but I want to visualize on a map before I say yes or not, and Mr. Clark said "that is all we want, we will put this on a map and we will bring it back to you and if you will O.K. it, then we can solve the problem.

Col. Bendetsen: Is Clark a reasonable man there?

General DeWitt: He is a very reasonable man.

9

"Resettlement Is Merely an Idea..."

Document 9†

February 5, 1942

MEMORANDUM FOR MR. McCLOY:

On Sunday, February 1, I understood from conversations with General DeWitt that his ideas might be expressed as I have expressed them in the following steps 1, 2, 3 and 4. Since then I have gained the impression that due to representations by Mr. Clark of the Department of Justice and, possibly, because of additional information, General DeWitt has changed his position in favor of more lenient treatment involving voluntary cooperation with Japanese-American citizen leaders. It is my view that such cooperation will be dangerous to rely upon and that the delay involved is extremely dangerous. I therefore recommend the following:

STEP 1

To declare restricted areas from which all alien enemies are excluded. This step has been begun and should be carried to completion.

STEP 2

Internment east of the Sierra Nevadas of *all* Japanese aliens, accompanied by such citizen members of their families as may volunteer for internment.

STEP 3

Change the nature of the restricted zones so as to make them, in effect, military reservations, to which admission will be granted only upon showing of proper credentials. As credentials would not be issued to citizens of Japanese extraction, this would result in excluding them from the restricted zones without raising too many legal questions.

STEP 4

In accordance with plans which may be developed by the Department of Agriculture, the Federal Security Administration, the Public Works Agency and other Government instrumentalities, to effect such resettlement and release from internment as may be possible and practicable, resettlement east of the Sierra Nevadas might be attempted. Resettlement is merely an idea and not an essential part of the plan.

ALLEN W. GULLION
Major General
Provost Marshal General

†From: Record Group 107, National Archives, Washington, D.C.

Document 9-a†

February 6, 1942.

MEMORANDUM for the Assistant Secretary of War.

If our production for war is seriously delayed by sabotage in the West Coastal states, we very possibly shall lose the war. I have not personally inspected the situation in those states, but from reliable reports from military and other sources, the danger of Japanese inspired sabotage is great. That danger cannot be temporized with. No half-way measures based upon considerations of economic disturbance, humanitarianism, or fear of retaliation will suffice. Such measures may be "too little and too late". Therefore, I recommend:

STEP 1

To declare restricted areas from which all alien enemies are excluded. This step has been begun and should be carried to completion.

STEP 2

Internment by the Army east of the Sierra Nevadas of *all* Japanese aliens, accompanied by such citizen members of their families as may volunteer for internment.

STEP 3

Change the nature of the restricted areas so as to make them, in effect, military reservations, to which admission will be granted only upon showing of proper credentials. As credentials would not be issued to citizens of Japanese extraction, this would result in excluding them from the restricted zones without raising too many legal questions.

STEP 4

In accordance with plans which may be developed by the Department of Agriculture, the Federal Security Administration, the Public Works Agency and other Government instrumentalities, to effect such resettlement and release from internment as may be possible and practicable, resettlement east of the Sierra Nevadas might be attempted. Resettlement is merely an idea, not an essential part of the plan, and not the function of the Army.

ALLEN W. GULLION,
Major General,
The Provost Marshal General.

†From: Record Group 107, National Archives, Washington, D.C.

10

The Expansion of Prohibited Areas

Document 10†

Department of Justice

[For immediate release Wednesday, February 4, 1942.]
Attorney General Francis Biddle announced today that the entire coast line of California from the Oregon border south to a point approximately 50 miles north of Los Angeles, and extending inland for distances varying from 30 to 150 miles, has been declared a "restricted area" for all alien enemies.

In addition, 11 other areas immediately surrounding certain hydroelectric generating plants throughout the State have also been placed in this category. Other restricted areas will be announced later as they are recommended by the War Department. The Attorney General has as yet received no recommendation from the War Department with respect to restricted areas for southern California.

The new regulation becomes effective on February 24, 1942. It provides as follows for all Japanese, German, and Italian aliens living in the restricted areas:

1. Between the hours of 9 p.m. and 6 a.m. all alien enemies shall be within the place of residence indicated on their certificates of identification.

2. At all other times during the day they must be found only at the place of residence or employment indicated in their certificates of identification, or going between those two places, or within a distance or not more than 5 miles from the place of residence.

3. Any alien enemy who is found during the hours of curfew at any place other than his place of residence or who is found during any other hour except at a place expressly specified as above, is subject to immediate apprehension and internment.

4. The United States attorneys will be authorized to grant exceptions to these restrictions only in cases where a compelling reason exists and after completion of a suitable investigation. While such an application is pending an alien enemy must comply with all of the restrictions. When exception is made to the restrictions, United States attorneys will endorse the exception in the

†From: U.S., Congress, House, Tolan Committee, 77th Cong., 2d sess., 1942, H. Rept. 2124.

certificate of identification so that the right of any alien enemy to be found in a restricted area may be immediately checked by examining his certificate, which he must have with him at all times.

The coastline region has been designated as restricted area No. 1. Its eastern boundary forms a line beginning at a point in Siskiyou County where United States Highway No. 99 crosses into Oregon, follows west and south generally along the lines of the Klamath and Trinity Rivers and on to approximately the town of Redwood Valley, in Mendocino County. At this point the boundary swings eastward just north of Clear Lake to Marysville, and then turns south to pass Sacramento and Stockton on the east and on to a point just south of Maricopa. The southern boundary of the area follows the line demarcating the northern and southern California military sectors, which runs eastward from a point on the coast near the boundary between San Luis Obispo and Santa Barbara Counties.

It is pointed out that regulations concerning "restricted" areas differ from those for "prohibited" areas, 86 of which have previously been designated by the Attorney General. Alien enemies are completely barred from prohibited areas. They may remain in the restricted areas but must observe the curfew and such other special regulations as may be announced. The fact that a prohibited area falls within the boundaries of a restricted area does not alter the rule that alien enemies are barred from prohibited areas.

However, particular alien enemies may be excluded entirely from these restricted areas whenever the Department of Justice deems such action necessary. Local police or other persons having information concerning particular alien enemies, indicating their presence within a restricted area might endanger the national security, should turn this information over to the Federal Bureau of Investigation. Prompt investigation will be made of every such complaint and the necessary action taken by the Attorney General.

11

The Problem of Legal Authority to Evacuate Citizens

Document 11†

Office of the Attorney General
Washington, D.C.

February 12, 1942

The Honorable
The Secretary of War
Washington, D.C.

My dear Mr. Secretary:

In further connection with my letter to you of February 9, with respect to the evacuation of Japanese from the West Coast, there seems to be a misunderstanding with respect to the responsibilities of the Army and the Department of Justice in connection therewith.

As I said in my letter of February 9, the proclamations issued by the President directing the Department of Justice to apprehend and evacuate alien enemies do not include American citizens of the Japanese race; therefore the Department of Justice has no power or authority to evacuate American-Japanese.

The question as to whether or not Japanese should be evacuated, whether citizens or not, necessarily involves a judgment based on military considerations. This, of course, is the responsibility of the Army. I have no doubt that the Army can legally, at any time, evacuate all persons in a specified territory if such action is deemed essential from a military point of view for the protection and defense of the area. No legal problem arises where Japanese citizens are evacuated; but American citizens of Japanese origin could not, in my opinion, be singled out of an area and evacuated with the other Japanese. However, the result might be accomplished by evacuating all persons in the area and then licensing back those whom the military authorities thought were not objectionable from a military point of view. These suggestions are made to you for your careful consideration in view of your prior recommendations and of the probable necessity of your taking further rigorous action.

---

†From: Record Group 107, National Archives, Washington, D.C.

Let me add again that the Department of Justice, and particularly the Federal Bureau of Investigation, is not staffed to undertake any evacuation on a large scale—larger, in fact, than has already been undertaken. Obviously the Army is the only organization which can arrange the evacuations.

These problems are so serious that I urge that you give them immediate and careful consideration.

You may, of course, count on the Department of Justice, under my direction, for advice and cooperation to the limit of our capacity.

Sincerely yours,
FRANCIS BIDDLE
Attorney General

Document 11-a†

[ca. February 11, 1942]

Draft

Questions to be determined re Japanese exclusion:

1. Is the President willing to authorize us to move Japanese citizens as well as enemy aliens from restricted areas.

2. Should we undertake withdrawal from the entire strip DeWitt originally recommended, which involves a number of over 100,000 people, if we included both aliens and Japanese citizens.

3. Should we undertake the intermediate step involving, say, 70,000, which includes large communities such as Los Angeles, San Diego, and Seattle.

4. Should we take any lesser step such as the establishment of restricted areas around airplane plants and critical installations, even though General DeWitt states that in several, at least, of the large communities this would be wasteful, involve difficult administrative problems, and might be a source of more continuous irritation and trouble than 100% withdrawal from the area.

General Gullion, the Provost Marshal General, has made the recommendations which are attached hereto. In substance they follow General DeWitt's intermediate recommendation.

General DeWitt recommends the intermediate plan and Colonel Bendetsen, who is now with General DeWitt, seems to take the same position. The removal will as a practical matter involve the setting up of shelter and food arrangements for a very large number of people and probably can only be undertaken by the Army. The Department of Justice refuses to take any steps which affect citizens unless in accordance with the usual legal processes which are impracticable if the objectives sought are to be obtained. The Department of Justice has also refused to go on with the evacuation even of enemy aliens from the large communities, on the ground that it involves too large a problem for them; and they also question the advisability or necessity of doing it unless all enemies are excluded from all the coastal cities, or at any rate they have asked for the reasons why the suggested removals from Seattle and Tacoma should take place.

†From: Record Group 107, National Archives, Washington, D.C.

12

"Eliminating the Possibility of Sabotage..."

Document 12†

14 February 1942

Subject: Evacuation of Japanese and other Subversive Persons from the Pacific Coast.

To: Commanding General, Field Forces
General Headquarters, Army War College
Washington, D.C.

1. There is inclosed herewith a memorandum for the Secretary of War in which the undersigned submits his recommendation on the above subject.

2. Such action, if taken, will be a positive step toward the elimination of the possibility of sabotage, espionage and subversive activities in this theater.

3. It must be understood that if the action recommended herein is approved by higher authority sufficient flexibility must be provided for the establishment of military areas additional to those which have been recommended to date, as may be found necessary from time to time as continuing study or events may dictate.

J.L. DeWITT
Lieutenant General, U.S. Army
Commanding

February 13, 1942

MEMORANDUM FOR: The Secretary of War
(Thru: The Commanding General,
Field Forces, Washington, D.C.)

SUBJECT: Evacuation of Japanese and other Subversive Persons from the Pacific Coast.

1. In presenting a recommendation for the evacuation of Japanese and other subversive persons from the Pacific Coast, the following facts have been considered:

---

†From: Record Group 107, National Archives, Washington, D.C.

a. Mission of the Western Defense Command and Fourth Army.

(1) Defense of the Pacific Coastal Frontier of the Western Defense Command, as extended, against attacks by sea, land or air;

(2) Local protection of establishments and communications vital to the National Defense for which adequate defense cannot be provided by local civilian authorities.

b. Brief Estimate of the Situation.

(1) Any estimate of the situation indicates that the following are possible and probable enemy activities:

(a) Naval attack on shipping in coastal waters;

(b) Naval attack on coastal cities and vital installations;

(c) Air raids on vital installations, particularly within two hundred miles of the coast;

(d) Sabotage of vital installations throughout the Western Defense Command.

Hostile Naval and air raids will be assisted by enemy agents signaling from the coastline and the vicinity thereof; and by supplying and otherwise assisting enemy vessels and by sabotage.

. . . .

b. I now recommend the following:

(1) That the Secretary of War procure from the President direction and authority to designate military areas in the combat zone of the Western Theater of Operations, (if necessary to include the entire combat zone), from which, in his discretion, he may exclude all Japanese, all alien enemies, and all other persons suspected for any reason by the administering military authorities of being actual or potential saboteurs, espionage agents, or fifth columnists. Such executive order should empower the Secretary of War to requisition the services of any and all other agencies of the Federal Government, with express direction to such agencies to respond to such requisition, and further empowering the Secretary of War to use any and all federal facilities and equipment, including CCC Camps, and to accept the use of State facilities for the purpose of providing shelter and equipment for evacuees. Such executive order to provide further for the administration of military areas for the purposes of this plan by appropriate military authorities acting with the requisitioned assistance of the other federal agencies and the cooperation of State and local agencies. The executive order should further provide that by reason of military necessity the right of all persons, whether citizens or aliens, to reside, enter, cross or be within any military areas shall be subject to revocation and shall exist on a pass and permit basis at the discretion of the Secretary of War and implemented by the necessary legislation imposing penalties for violation.

(2) That, pursuant to such executive order, there be designated as military areas all areas in Washington, Oregon and California, recommended by me to date for designation by the Attorney General as Category "A" areas and such additional areas as it may be found necessary to designate hereafter.

(3) That the Secretary of War provide for the exclusion from such military areas, in his discretion, of the following classes of persons viz.:

(*a*) Japanese aliens.

(*b*) Japanese American citizens.

(*c*) Alien enemies other than Japanese aliens.

(*d*) Any and all other persons who are suspected for any reason by the administering military authorities to be actual or potential saboteurs, espionage agents, fifth columnists, or subversive persons.

(4) That the evacuation of classes (*a*), (*b*), and (*c*) from such military areas be initiated on a designated evacuation day and carried to completion as rapidly as practicable.

That prior to evacuation day all plans be complete for the establishment of initial concentration points, reception centers, registration, rationing, guarding, transportation to internment points, and the selection and establishment of internment facilities in the Sixth, Seventh, and Eighth Corps Areas.

That persons in class (*a*) and (*c*) above be evacuated and interned at such selected places of internment, under guard.

That persons in class (*b*) above, at the time of evacuation, be offered an opportunity to accept voluntary internment, under guard, at the places of internment above mentioned.

That those persons in class (*b*) who decline to accept voluntary internment, be excluded from all military areas, and left to their own resources, or, in the alternative, be encouraged to accept resettlement outside of such military areas with such assistances as the State governments concerned or the Federal Security Agency may be by that time prepared to offer. . . .

J.L. DeWITT,
Lieutenant General, U.S. Army,
Commanding.

13

"A Closely Guarded Secret"

Document 13†

February 17, 1942.

IMMEDIATE ACTION

MEMORANDUM for The Adjutant General.

Subject: Evacuation of Japanese from West Coast.

1. It is requested that an urgent secret radiogram be dispatched over the signature of The Adjutant General to the Commanders, all Corps Areas, substantially as follows:

TO: COMMANDING GENERAL ALL CORPS AREAS

SUBJECT: EVACUATION OF JAPANESE FROM PACIFIC COAST

PROBABLE THAT ORDERS FOR VERY LARGE EVACUATION OF ENEMY ALIENS OF ALL NATIONALITIES PREDOMINENTLY JAPANESE FROM PACIFIC COAST WILL ISSUE WITHIN FORTY EIGHT HOURS PERIOD INTERNMENT FACILITIES WILL BE TAXED TO UTMOST PERIOD REPORT AT ONCE MAXIMUM YOU CAN CARE FOR COMMA INCLUDING HOUSING COMMA FEEDING COMMA MEDICAL CARE AND SUPPLY PERIOD YOUR BREAK DOWN SHOULD INCLUDE NUMBER OF MEN COMMA WOMEN AND CHILDREN STOP VERY IMPORTANT TO KEEP THIS A CLOSELY GUARDED SECRET END

ADAMS

ACTION TAKEN: BY
radio to CG, 1ST
CORPS AREA, and all
CORPS AREAS. 2-17-42
EHB/cdm—1705

ALLEN W. GULLION,
Major General, U.S. Army,
The Provost Marshal General.

14

The Right to Relocate Citizens: The Delegation of Authority

Document 14†

Executive Order—No. 9066

WHEREAS the successful prosecution of the war requires every possible protection against espionage and against sabotage to national defense material, national defense premises, and national defense utilities as defined in Section 4, Act of April 20, 1918, 40 Stat. 533, as amended by the Act of November 30, 1940, 54 Stat. 1220, and the Act of August 21, 1941, 55 Stat. 655 (U.S.C., Title 50, Sec. 104):

Now, THEREFORE, by virtue of the authority vested in me as President of the United States, and Commander in Chief of the Army and Navy, I hereby authorize and direct the Secretary of War, and the Military Commanders who he may from time to time designate, whenever he or any designated Commander deems such action necessary or desirable, to prescribe military areas in such places and of such extent as he or the appropriate Military Commander may determine, from which any or all persons may be excluded, and with respect to which, the right of any person to enter, remain in, or leave shall be subject to whatever restrictions the Secretary of War or the appropriate Military Commander may impose in his discretion. The Secretary of War is hereby authorized to provide for residents of any such area who are excluded therefrom, such transportation, food, shelter, and other accommodations as may be necessary, in the judgment of the Secretary of War or the said Military Commander, and until other arrangements are made, to accomplish the purpose of this order. The designation of military-areas in any region or locality shall supersede designations of prohibited and restricted areas by the Attorney General under the Proclamations of December 7 and 8, 1941, and shall supersede the responsibility and authority of the Attorney

†From: U.S., Congress, House, Tolan Committee, 77th Cong., 2d sess., 1942, H. Rept. 2124.

113

General under the said Proclamations in respect of such prohibited and restricted areas.

I hereby further authorize and direct the Secretary of War and the said Military Commanders to take such other steps as he or the appropriate Military Commander may deem advisable to enforce compliance with the restrictions applicable to each Military area hereinabove authorized to be designated, including the use of Federal troops and other Federal Agencies, with authority to accept assistance of state and local agencies.

I hereby further authorize and direct all Executive Departments, independent establishments and other Federal Agencies, to assist the Secretary of War or the said Military Commanders in carrying out this Executive Order, including the furnishing of medical aid, hospitalization, food, clothing, transportation, use of land, shelter, and other supplies, equipment, utilities, facilities, and services.

This order shall not be construed as modifying or limiting in any way the authority heretofore granted under Executive Order No. 8972, dated December 12, 1941, nor shall it be construed as limiting or modifying the duty and responsibility of the Federal Bureau of Investigation, with respect to the investigation of alleged acts of sabotage or the duty and responsibility of the Attorney General and the Department of Justice under the Proclamations of December 7 and 8, 1941, prescribing regulations for the conduct and control of alien enemies, except as such duty and responsibility is superseded by the designation of military areas hereunder.

THE WHITE HOUSE,
February 19, 1942.

Document 14-a†

WAR DEPARTMENT
Office of the Provost Marshal General

Aliens Division   February 20, 1942.
PMG 014.311

MEMORANDUM for the Chief of Staff.
Subject: Control of Alien Enemies and other Subversive Persons on the Pacific Coast.

This is in reference to your request for a summary of developments regarding the above subject.

1. The initial approach to the problem was on an alien enemy basis. The Attorney General stated that he did not have facilities to undertake a study for the purpose of designating areas prohibited to alien enemies surrounding vital installations. Accordingly, the Army submitted recommendations and these were in turn adopted in part by The Attorney General. In 88 areas in California alien enemies are now under an exclusion order with a February 24 deadline.

†From: Record Group 107, National Archives, Washington, D.C.

2. Progressively it became apparent that some means would have to be devised to control dangerous citizens as well as aliens; that there was as much to be feared from American citizens of Japanese lineage as from Japanese aliens. The Attorney General took the position that the Justice Department could not handle American citizens by excluding them from or denying them access to strategic areas under any conditions. Accordingly, the Secretary of War obtained a verbal commitment from the President that he (The President) would direct the necessary action to designate military areas, with power to exclude any or all persons therefrom and to control their movements therein. The Secretary of War (through Lt. Colonel Bendetsen) called for General DeWitt's recommendations for the course of action to pursue under such authority. Accordingly, General DeWitt recommended in brief, that the following areas along the Pacific Coast be designated as military areas:

    a. San Diego.

    b. Los Angeles.

    c. San Francisco, including the entire bay district.

    d. That portion of the Washington state lying west of the Cascade.

    e. The northwest corner of Oregon state west of the Cascade.

    f. A strip along the Pacific Coast 15 miles in width.

General DeWitt proposed the complete exclusion from zones within that area of all Japanese including American citizens and of all alien enemies.

3. An Executive Order was prepared for the signature of the President and signed by the President February 19. (Tab A) This order gives the authority necessary to carry out General DeWitt's recommendations and take similar steps anywhere in the United States. Either the Secretary of War, or any Military Commander whom the Secretary of War designates, is empowered to prescribe military areas in such places and of such extent as the Administering Authority may determine.

4. Accordingly, but without expressly adopting General DeWitt's recommendation, the Secretary of War designated General DeWitt as the military commander to carry out the Executive Order in the Western Defense Command. (Tab B) The Order of the Secretary of War was read to and concurred in by authorized representatives of all divisions of the War Department General Staff. In essence, General DeWitt's authority under the executive authority is limited only by the restriction on the number of troops available to him to undertake evacuation.

5. The probable outline of action is as shown in the accompanying outline memorandum. (Tab C) General DeWitt advises that he proposes to designate as military areas those areas listed above, to provide progressively for exclusion of all Japanese, initially only around the most critical areas, making full use of whatever voluntary exodus that private impetus and recognized relief agencies can stimulate. He plans, of course, in so doing to supersede the areas designated by The Attorney General and thus acquire full control of all subversive elements and classes in all of those areas.

ALLEN W. GULLION,
Major General, U.S. Army,
The Provost Marshal General.

Document 14-b†

February 20, 1942.

Commanding General,
Western Defense Command and Fourth Army,
Presidio of San Francisco, California.

Dear General DeWitt:

By Executive Order, dated February 19, 1942, copy inclosed, the President authorized and directed me, through the Military Commander whom I designate, to prescribe military areas for the protection of vital installations against sabotage and espionage. The cited Executive Order also authorized and directed the administering authority to impose such restrictions upon the right to enter, remain in, or leave any such areas as may be appropriate to the requirements in each instance. Accordingly, I designate you as the Military Commander to carry out the duties and responsibilities imposed by said Executive Order for that portion of the United States embraced in the Western Defense Command, including such changes in the prohibited and restricted areas heretofore designated by The Attorney General as you deem proper to prescribe.

In carrying out your duties under this delegation, I desire, so far as military requirements permit, that you do not disturb, for the time being at least, Italian aliens and persons of Italian lineage except where they are, in your judgment, undesirable or constitute a definite danger to the performance of your mission to defend the West Coast. I ask that you take this action in respect to Italians for the reason that I consider such persons to be potentially less dangerous, as a whole, than those of other enemy nationalities. Because of the size of the Italian population and the number of troops and facilities which would have to be employed to deal with them, their inclusion in the general plan would greatly overtax our strength. In this connection it may be necessary for you to relieve Italian aliens from the necessity for compliance with The Attorney General's order respecting the California prohibited areas 1 to 88 (Category A). This may appropriately be done by designating, sufficiently in advance of February 24, the said areas as military areas and by excepting Italian aliens from the classes excluded.

With due regard to your other missions you may use the troops you can now make available from your general command, but for this purpose the 27th Division and the 3rd Division reinforced are not to be considered as part of your general command as such troops are assigned to your command only for specific training.

Your attention is invited to those provisions of the Executive Order under which you are authorized to call for assistance, supplies, and services from all Government agencies. It is desired that you take full advantage of that authority.

†From: Record Group 107, National Archives, Washington, D.C.

Removal of individuals from areas in which they are domiciled should be accomplished gradually so as to avoid, so far as is consistent with national safety and the performance of your mission, unnecessary hardship and dislocation of business and industry. In order to permit the War Department to make plans for the proper disposition of individuals whom you contemplate moving outside of your jurisdiction, it is desired that you make known to me your detailed plans for evacuation. Individuals will not be entrained until such plans are furnished and you are informed that accommodations have been prepared at the point of detraining.

So far as practicable, fullest advantage should be taken of voluntary exodus of individuals and of the facilities afforded by other Government and private agencies in assisting evacuees to resettle. Where evacuees are unable to effect resettlement of their own volition, or with the assistance of other agencies, proper provision for housing, feeding, transportation and medical care must be provided.

I desire that from time to time you make report direct to me of important actions and events, particularly with respect to the extent and location of military areas, and the restrictions applicable thereto.

Sincerely yours,
HENRY L. STIMSON
Secretary of War.

Document 14-c†

February 20, 1942

OUTLINE MEMORANDUM [Stimson to DeWitt]

By Executive Order, dated February 19, 1942, the President authorized and directed me, through the Military Commander whom I designate, to prescribe military areas for the protection of vital installations against sabotage and espionage. The cited Executive Order authorizes and directs the Administering Authority to impose such restrictions upon the right to enter, remain in, or leave any such areas as may be appropriate to the requirements in each instance. Accordingly, I designate you as the Military Commander to carry out the duties and responsibilities imposed by said Executive Order for that portion of the United States embraced in the Western Defense Command, including such changes in prohibited and restricted areas already designated by the Attorney General, as you may deem prudent.

For the purposes of these instructions, persons resident in the Western Defense Command will be classified as follows:

Class 1 Japanese Aliens
Class 2 American citizens of Japanese Lineage
Class 3 German Aliens
Class 4 Italian Aliens

Class 5 Any persons, whether citizens or aliens, who are suspected for any reason by you or your responsible subordinates, of being actually or potentially dangerous either as saboteurs, espionage agents, fifth-columnists or subversive persons.

Class 6 All other persons who are, or who may be within Western Defense Command.

As soon as practicable you will designate military areas in such places and of such extent in the Western Defense Command as in your judgment will afford the maximum protection to those installations, facilities, plants, and utilities situated within your Command meet vital to the war effort. From these areas you will provide for the exclusion of all persons in Classes 1, 2, 3, and 5.

You will note from the contents of the Executive Order that the designation by you of any military area inclusive of any prohibited or restricted area previously promulgated by the Attorney General under the Presidential Proclamations of December 7 and 8, 1941, supersedes any such previously designated prohibited and restricted areas. The Attorney General has designated a number of prohibited and restricted areas in the State of California corresponding to certain of the recommendations heretofore submitted by you through the Secretary of War to the Attorney General. The areas already designated by The Attorney General as prohibited and restricted areas are the Category "A" areas, numbered 1-88 and the Category "B" areas, 1-12, in California. As alien enemies residing in military areas designated as prohibited areas (recommended by you as Category "A" areas) are now under an order of the Attorney General to evacuate not later than February 24, 1942, it is recommended that you proceed without delay, as an initial step in your program, to re-designate the prohibited areas (Category "A" areas) shown on the inclosed list as military areas. It is desired that you take appropriate measures to permit Italian alien enemies to remain in those areas for the present, at least during good behaviour, excluding only those Italian alien enemies who are individually suspect, viz. who are in Class 5.

With respect to the restricted areas (recommended by you as Category "B" areas) heretofore designated by The Attorney General in the State of California, you are aware that certain restrictive regulations applicable to alien enemies resident therein have been promulgated by the Department of Justice. These restrictive regulations have no application to persons other than alien enemies whose movements you might deem it necessary to restrict. Further, alien enemies excluded by order of The Attorney General from prohibited areas (Category "A" areas) may not re-settle themselves in restricted areas (Category "B" areas) without express permission. However, should you supersede the California prohibited areas (Category "A" areas) already designated by The Attorney General and provide for the exclusion of Classes 1 and 2 therefrom, the American citizen of Japanese lineage could re-settle in any restricted area (Category "B" areas) unless you prescribe a military area or areas coincident with the restricted areas (Category "B" areas) already designated.

I suggest the advisability of the following course of action:

1. The designation by you of a military area in California coincident with restricted area number one.

2. The designation by you of prohibited zones within that military area coincident with California (Category "A") prohibited areas number 1 to 88 inclusive.

3. The exclusion of Classes 1 and 3 from the zones referred to in 2 above on or before February 24, 1942, for the exclusion of Class 2 from the zones referred to within a time to be limited by you in each instance or by your responsible subordinate. In this connection, reference is made to the comments hereinafter set forth pertinent to the determination of effective dates of exclusion.

4. The exclusion of all persons in Class 5 as soon as practicable, including in Class 5 any Class 4 persons who are individually suspect.

5. The promulgation of appropriate restrictions controlling movement through or within the zones referred to in 2 above, as well as through or within the entire military area.

6. Except with your express permission in each instance, or with the permission of your responsible subordinate, any persons excluded from any of the zones referred to in 2 above should be excluded from the entire California military area, viz., the military area referred to in 1 above.

7. The progressive designation by you of military areas throughout the Western Defense Command of such extent and in such places as you deem necessary to provide the maximum protection from sabotage and espionage of installations vital to the war effort consistent with the means available for evacuation and the military responsibilities attendant upon evacuation of large numbers of persons.

8. Where necessary, in your judgment, the designation of protective zones within the military areas referred to in 7 above, in which you will provide (a) for the exclusion of all persons in Classes 1, 2 and 5, and where in your judgment it is essential, and (b) for the exclusion of persons in Class 3, so as to afford the maximum protection from espionage and sabotage to installations vital to the war effort, consistent with the military responsibilities attendant upon such an evacuation, viz., the number of troops which will be diverted from training for combat and from other missions, the fulfillment of which is your responsibility.

9. The promulgation of appropriate restrictive regulations governing the exercise by any person of the right to enter, remain in or leave such military areas and any zones within such military areas. In connection with the initiation, development and accomplishment of the program outlined above, you will initiate and carry to completion, without delay, the preparation of detailed plans for the evacuation of those classes of persons and individuals who will be excluded from military areas prescribed by you. In so doing it is desired that you take full

advantage of the provisions of the Executive Order whereby you are authorized to call upon the other executive departments and federal agencies for assistance, not only in the furnishing of services, but also of supplies, equipment and land. It is the intention that the heads of the several executive departments, independent establishments, and other federal agencies will be required and will have full authority to respond to such requests as you may make upon them in carrying out the provisions of the executive order.

10. In this connection so far as consistent with safety the development of your program should be by stages. In the most critical areas as you may consider it necessary to bring about an almost immediate evacuation of certain classes, particularly classes 1 and 2. However, in order to take full advantage of voluntary exodus and of re-settlement facilities arranged by other agencies, both public and private, the timing of your program should be most carefully conceived and coordinated. Representatives of the Department of Justice and Agriculture advise that in those instances where it is consistent with the safety to afford evacuees reasonable advance notice that they will be able greatly to decrease the numbers of evacuees to be cared for by the Army, and thereby greatly decrease the drain on our military resources; thus avoiding the diversion of troops from their primary mission, the defense of the West Coast.

11. In providing for the exclusion of classes of persons and individuals from military areas prescribed by you, you will make appropriate exception in favor of the aged, infirm, and the sick. Persons above the age of 70 years should not be disturbed unless for sufficient reason, you consider them suspect. Unless you find that the national safety will not so permit, bona fida refugees in Class 3 should be afforded special consideration, either through the development of suitable means to acquire permits to return to prohibited zones or to remain therein.

12. It [?] I desire that you make known to me your detailed plans for evacuation as soon as practicable in order to enable the War Department to coordinate with the Corps Area Commanders concerned any movement you propose to undertake of evacuees outside of your command to places of temporary shelter. You will not entrain any evacuees for transportation beyond your command until you have been informed by the War Department that accommodations are prepared to receive them at the places of destination.

13. Yours will be the military responsibility for processing, evacuation, supplying, rationing and transportation to the points of shelter. This, of course, applies only to those evacuees who are unable to re-settle themselves on their own resources or for whom public and private agencies have been unable to arrange resettlement. For persons in this class, the Army will provide shelter, food and other accommodations,

including medical aid and hospitalization selected places in the interior until civil authorities can make other arrangements.

14. It will be the military responsibility of the Corps Area Commanders to prepare those accommodations and to undertake their supply and administration. For the purpose of accomplishing the necessary arrangements, direct communication between you and the Corps Area Commanders concerned is authorized. You will furnish the War Department with copies of all direct communications between you and the Corps Area Commanders.

15. It will, of course, be necessary that your plans include provision for protection of the property, particularly the physical property, of evacuees. All reasonable measures should be taken through publicity and other means, to encourage evacuees to take steps to protect their own property. Where evacuees are unable to do this prior to the time when it is necessary for them to comply with exclusion orders, there is always danger that unscrupulous persons will take undue advantage or that physical property unavoidably left behind will be pillaged by lawless elements. The protection of physical property from theft or other harm is primarily the responsibility of state and local law-enforcement agencies, and you will doubtless call upon them for the maximum assistance in this connection. Where they are unable to protect physical property left behind in military areas, the responsibility will be yours, to provide reasonable protection, either through the use of troops or through other appropriate measures. The appointment by you of a property custodian and the creation by him of an organization to deal with such property in military areas may become necessary. The provisions of the Executive Order and the necessity in each given instance are such that you have authority to take such action, either directly or through another federal agency. In the development of your program, it is desired that you accomplish it with the minimum of individual hardship and dislocation of business and industries consistent with safety. Report to me from time to time by telephone, with confirmation in writing, of important action and comments, indicating particularly the location and extent of military areas prescribed by you and the character of the restrictions promulgated.

16. With due regard to your other missions in the discharge of your authorities and responsibilities under the cited Executive Order, you may use any of the troops of your command now available to you, less the 27 Division and the 3rd Division reinforced.

Sincerely yours,
HENRY L. STIMSON
Secretary of War.

15

Regulations Governing the Conduct of All Enemy Aliens and Japanese Citizens: De Witt Exercises His Authority

Document 15†

Public Proclamation No. 5

Headquarters, Western Defense Command and Fourth Army,
Presidio of San Francisco, California, March 30, 1942.
To the people within the States of Washington, Oregon, California, Montana, Idaho, Nevada, Utah, and Arizona, and the Public Generally:

WHEREAS, by Public Proclamation No. 1, dated March 2, 1942, this headquarters, there were designated and established Military Areas Nos. 1 and 2 and Zones thereof, and

WHEREAS, by Public Proclamation No. 2, dated March 16, 1942, this headquarters, there were designated and established Military Areas Nos. 3, 4, 5, and 6 and Zones thereof, and

WHEREAS, the present situation within these Military Areas and Zones requires as a matter of military necessity the establishment of certain regulations, as set forth hereinafter:

NOW, THEREFORE, I, J.L. DE WITT, Lieutenant General, U.S. Army, by virtue of the authority vested in me by the President of the United States and by the Secretary of War and my powers and prerogatives as Commanding

†From: U.S., Congress, House, Tolan Committee, 77th Cong., 2d sess., 1942, H. Rept. 2124.

General, Western Defense Command, do hereby declare and establish the following regulations covering the conduct to be observed by all alien Japanese, all alien Germans, all alien Italians, and all persons of Japanese ancestry residing or being within the Military Areas above described:

Prior to and during the period of exclusion and evacuation of certain persons or classes of persons from prescribed Military Areas and Zones, persons otherwise subject thereto but who come within one or more of the classes specified in *(a)*, *(b)*, *(c)*, *(d)*, *(e)*, and *(f)*, following, may make written application for exemption from such exclusion and evacuation. Application Form WDC—PM 5 has been prepared for that purpose and copies thereof may be procured from any United States Post Office or United States Employment Service office in the Western Defense Command by persons who deem themselves entitled to exemption.

The following classes of persons are hereby authorized to be exempted from exclusion and evacuation upon the furnishing of satisfactory proof as specified in Form WDC—PM 5:

(a) German and Italian aliens seventy or more years of age.

(b) In the case of German and Italian aliens, the parent, wife, husband, child of (or other person who resides in the household and whose support is wholly dependent upon) an officer, enlisted man or commissioned nurse on active duty in the Army of the United States (or any component thereof), U.S. Navy, U.S. Marine Corps, or U.S. Coast Guard.

(c) In the case of German and Italian aliens, the parent, wife, husband, child of (or other person who resides in the household and whose support is wholly dependent upon) an officer, enlisted man or commissioned nurse who on or since December 7, 1941, died in line of duty with the armed services of the United States indicated in the preceding subparagraph.

(d) German and Italian aliens awaiting naturalization who had filed a petition for naturalization and who had paid the filing fee therefor in a court of competent jurisdiction on or before December 7, 1941.

(e) Patients in hospital, or confined elsewhere, and too ill or incapacitated to be removed therefrom without danger to life.

(f) Inmates of orphanages and the totally deaf, dumb, or blind.

The applicant for exemption will be required to furnish the kinds of proof specified in Form WDC—PM 5 in support of the application. The certificate of exemption from evacuation will also include exemption from compliance with curfew regulations, subject, however, to such future proclamations or orders in the premises as may from time to time be issued by this headquarters. The person to whom such exemption from evacuation and curfew has been granted shall thereafter be entitled to reside in any portion of any prohibited area, including those areas heretofore declared prohibited by the Attorney General of the United States.

J.L. DeWITT,
Lieutenant General, U.S. Army,
Commanding.

Document 15-a†

Public Proclamation No. 3

Headquarters, Western Defense Command and Fourth Army,
Presidio of San Francisco, California, March 24, 1942.
To the people within the States of Washington, Oregon, California, Montana,
Idaho, Nevada, Utah and Arizona, and the Public Generally:

WHEREAS, By Public Proclamation No. 1, dated March 2, 1942, this headquarters, there were designated and established Military Areas Nos. 1 and 2 and Zones thereof, and

WHEREAS, By Public Proclamation No. 2, dated March 16, 1942, this headquarters, there were designated and established Military Areas Nos. 3, 4, 5, and 6 and Zones thereof, and

WHEREAS, The present situation within these Military Areas and Zones requires as a matter of military necessity the establishment of certain regulations pertaining to all enemy aliens and all persons of Japanese ancestry within said Military Areas and Zones thereof:

NOW, THEREFORE I, J.L. DEWITT, Lieutenant General, U.S. Army, by virtue of the authority vested in me by the President of the United States and by the Secretary of War and my powers and prerogatives as Commanding General, Western Defense Command, do hereby declare and establish the following regulations covering the conduct to be observed by all alien Japanese, all alien Germans, all alien Italians, and all persons of Japanese ancestry residing or being within the Military Areas above described, or such portions thereof as are hereinafter mentioned:

1. From and after 6:00 A.M., March 27, 1942, all alien Japanese, all alien Germans, all alien Italians, and all persons of Japanese ancestry residing or being within the geographical limits of Military Area No. 1, or within any of the Zones established within Military Area No. 2, as those areas are defined and described in Public Proclamation No. 1, dated March 2, 1942, this headquarters, or within the geographical limits of the designated Zones established within Military Areas Nos. 3, 4, 5, and 6, as those areas are defined and described in Public Proclamation No. 2, dated March 16, 1942, this headquarters, or within any of such additional Zones as may hereafter be similarly designated and defined, shall be within their place of residence between the hours of 8:00 P.M. and 6:00 A.M., which period is hereinafter referred to as the hours of curfew.

2. At all other times all such persons shall be only at their place of residence or employment or traveling between those places or within a distance of not more than five miles from their place of residence.

3. Nothing in paragraph 2 shall be construed to prohibit any of the above specified persons from visiting the nearest United States Post Office, United States Employment Service Office, or office operated or maintained by the

†From: U.S., Congress, House, Tolan Committee, 77th Cong., 2d sess., 1942, H. Rept. 2124.

Wartime Civil Control Administration, for the purpose of transacting any business or the making of any arrangement reasonably necessary to accomplish evacuation; nor be construed to prohibit travel under duly issued change of residence notice and travel permit provided for in paragraph 5 of Public Proclamation Numbers 1 and 2. Travel performed in change of residence to a place outside the prohibited and restricted areas may be performed without regard to curfew hours.

4. Any person violating these regulations will be subject to immediate exclusion from the Military Areas and Zones specified in paragraph 1 and to the criminal penalties provided by Public Law No. 503, 77th Congress, approved March 21, 1942, entitled: "An Act to Provide a Penalty for Violation of Restrictions or Orders With Respect to Persons Entering, Remaining in, Leaving or Committing Any Act in Military Areas or Zone." In the case of any alien enemy, such person will in addition be subject to immediate apprehension and internment.

5. By subsequent proclamation or order there will be prescribed those classes of persons who will be entitled to apply for exemptions from exclusion orders hereafter to be issued. Persons granted such exemption will likewise and at the same time also be exempted from the operation of the curfew regulations of this proclamation.

6. After March 31, 1942, no person of Japanese ancestry shall have in his possession or use or operate at any time or place within any of the Military Areas 1 to 6 inclusive, as established and defined in Public Proclamations Nos. 1 and 2, above mentioned any of the following items:

(a) Firearms.
(b) Weapons or implements of war or component parts thereof.
(c) Ammunition.
(d) Bombs.
(e) Explosives or the component parts thereof.
(f) Short-wave radio receiving sets having a frequency of 1,750 kilocycles or greater or of 540 kilocycles or less.
(g) Radio transmitting sets.
(h) Signal devices.
(i) Codes or ciphers.
(j) Cameras.

Any such person found in possession of any of the above named items in violation of the foregoing will be subject to the criminal penalties provided by Public Law No. 503, 77th Congress, approved March 21, 1942, entitled: "An Act to Provide a Penalty for Violation of Restrictions or Orders with Respect to Persons Entering Remaining in, Leaving or Committing Any Act in Military Areas or Zone."

7. The regulations herein prescribed with reference to the observance of curfew hours by enemy aliens, are substituted for and supersede the regulations of the United States Attorney General heretofore in force in certain limited areas. All curfew exemptions heretofore granted by the United

States Attorneys are hereby revoked effective as of 6:00 a.m., PWT, March, 27, 1942.

8. The Federal Bureau of Investigation is designated as the agency to enforce the foregoing provisions. It is requested that the civil police within the states affecting by this Proclamation assist the Federal Bureau of Investigation by reporting to it the names and addresses of all persons believed to have violated these regulations.

J.L. DeWITT,
Lieutenant General,
U.S. Army, Commanding.

Document 15-b†

Civilian Exclusion Order No. 1

Headquarters, Western Defense Command and Fourth Army,
Presidio of San Francisco, California, March 24, 1942.

1. Pursuant to the provision of Public Proclamations Nos. 1 and 2, this headquarters, dated March 2, 1942, and March 16, 1942, respectively, it is hereby ordered that all persons of Japanese ancestry, including aliens and nonaliens, be excluded from that portion of Military Area No. 1 described as "Bainbridge Island," in the State of Washington, on or before 12 o'clock noon, P.W.T., of the 30th day of March 1942.

2. Such exclusion will be accomplished in the following manner:

(a) Such persons may, with permission, on or prior to March 29, 1942, proceed to any approved place of their choosing beyond the limits of Military Area No. 1 and the prohibited zones established by said proclamations or hereafter similarly established, subject only to such regulations as to travel and change of residence as are now or may hereafter be prescribed by this headquarters and by the United States Attorney General. Persons affected hereby will not be permitted to take up residence or remain within the region designated as Military Area No. 1 or the prohibited zones heretofore or hereafter established. Persons affected hereby are required on leaving or entering Bainbridge Island to register and obtain a permit at the Civil Control Office to be established on said Island at or near the ferryboat landing.

(b) On March 30, 1942, all such persons who have not removed themselves from Bainbridge Island in accordance with Paragraph 1 hereof shall, in accordance with instructions of the Commanding General, Northwestern Sector, report to the Civil Control Office referred to above on Bainbridge Island for evacuation in such manner and to such place or places as shall then be prescribed.

(c) A responsible member of each family affected by this order and each individual living alone so affected will report to the Civil Control Office described above between 8 a.m. and 5 p.m. Wednesday, March 25, 1942.

†From: U.S., Congress, House, Tolan Committee, 77th Cong., 2d sess., 1942, H. Rept. 2124.

3. Any person affected by this order who fails to comply with any of its provisions or who is found on Bainbridge Island after 12 o'clock noon, P.W.T., of March 30, 1942, will be subject to the criminal penalties provided by Public Law No. 503, 77th Congress, approved March 21, 1942, entitled "An Act to Provide a Penalty for Violation of Restrictions or Orders with Respect to Persons Entering, Remaining in, Leaving, or Committing Any Act in Military Areas or Zone", and alien Japanese will be subject to immediate apprehension and internment.

J.L. DeWitt,
Lieutenant General, U.S. Army,
Commanding.

Instructions to All Japanese Living on Bainbridge Island

All Japanese persons, both alien and nonalien, will be evacuated from this area by twelve noon, Monday, March 30, 1942.

No Japanese person will be permitted to leave or enter Bainbridge Island after 9:00 a.m., March 24, 1942, without obtaining special permission from the Civil Control Office established on this island near the ferryboat landing at the Anderson Dock Store in Winslow.

The Civil Control Office is equipped to assist the Japanese population affected by this evacuation in the following ways:

1. Give advice and instructions on the evacuation.

2. Provide services with respect to the management, leasing, sale, storage, or other disposition of most kinds of property, including farms, livestock and farm equipment, boats, tools, household goods, automobiles, etc.

3. Provide temporary residence for all Japanese in family groups, elsewhere.

4. Transport persons and a limited amount of clothing and equipment to their new residence, as specified below.

5. Give medical examinations and make provision for all invalided persons affected by the evacuation order.

6. Give special permission to individuals and families who are able to leave the area and proceed to an approved destination of their own choosing on or prior to March 29, 1942.

The following instructions must be observed:

1. A responsible member of each family, preferably the head of the family, or the person in whose name most of the property is held, and each individual living alone, will report to the Civil Control Office to receive further instruction. This must be done between 8:00 a.m. and 5:00 p.m., Wednesday, March 25, 1942.

2. Before leaving the area all persons will be given a medical examination. For this purpose all members of the family should be present at the same time when directed by the Civil Control Office.

Document 15-c†

Public Proclamation No. 4

No. 18

Headquarters, Western Defense Command and Fourth Army,

Presidio of San Francisco, California, March 27, 1942.

To the people within the States of Washington, Oregon, California, Montana, Idaho, Nevada, Utah and Arizona, and the Public Generally:

WHEREAS, By Public Proclamation No. 1, dated March 2, 1942, this headquarters, there was designated and established Military Area No. 1, and

WHEREAS, It is necessary, in order to provide for the welfare and to insure the orderly evacuation and resettlement of Japanese voluntarily migrating from Military Area No. 1, to restrict and regulate such migration:

NOW, THEREFORE, I, J.L. DEWITT, Lieutenant General, U.S. Army, by virtue of the authority vested in me by the President of the United States and by the Secretary of War and my powers and prerogatives as Commanding General, Western Defense Command, do hereby declare that the present situation requires as a matter of military necessity that, commencing at 12:00 midnight, P.W.T., March 29, 1942, all alien Japanese and persons of Japanese ancestry who are within the limits of Military Area No. 1, be and they are hereby prohibited from leaving that area for any purpose until and to the extent that a future proclamation or order of this headquarters shall so permit or direct.

Any person violating this proclamation will be subject to the criminal penalties provided by Public Law No. 503, 77th Congress, approved March 21, 1942, entitled: "An Act to Provide a Penalty for Violation of Restrictions or Orders with Respect to Persons Entering, Remaining in, Leaving or Committing Any Act in Military Areas or Zones." In the case of any alien enemy, such person will in addition be subject to immediate apprehension and internment.

J.L. DeWITT,
Lieutenant General,
U.S. Army, Commanding.

†From: U.S., Congress, House, Tolan Committee, 77th Cong., 2d sess., 1942, H. Rept. 2124.

16

The Emergency Detention Act of 1950

Document 16†

Title II—Emergency Detention

Short Title

Sec. 100. This title may be cited as the "Emergency Detention Act of 1950".

Findings of Fact and Declaration of Purpose

Sec. 101. As a result of evidence adduced before various committees of the Senate and the House of Representatives, the Congress hereby finds that—

(1) There exists a world Communist movement which in its origins, its development, and its present practice, is a world-wide revolutionary movement whose purpose it is, by treachery, deceit, infiltration into other groups (governmental and otherwise), espionage, sabotage, terrorism, and any other means deemed necessary, to establish a Communist totalitarian dictatorship in all the countries of the world through the medium of a world-wide Communist organization.

. . . .

(13) The recent successes of Communist methods in other countries and the nature and control of the world Communist movement itself present a clear and present danger to the security of the United States and to the existence of free American institutions, and make it necessary that Congress, in order to provide for the common defense, to preserve the sovereignty of the United States as an independent nation, and to guarantee to each State a republican form of government, enact appropriate legislation recognizing the existence of such world-wide conspiracy and designed to prevent it from accomplishing its purpose in the United States.

(14) The detention of persons who there is reasonable ground to believe probably will commit or conspire with others to commit espionage or sabotage is, in a time of internal security emergency, essential to the common defense and to the safety and security of the territory, the people and the Constitution of the United States.

(15) It is also essential that such detention in an emergency involving the internal security of the Nation shall be so authorized, executed, restricted and

†From: U.S. *Statutes at Large*, vol. 64, p. 1019.

reviewed as to prevent any interference with the constitutional rights and privileges of any persons, and at the same time shall be sufficiently effective to permit the performance by the Congress and the President of their constitutional duties to provide for the common defense, to wage war, and to preserve, protect and defend the Constitution, the Government and the people of the United States.

Declaration of "Internal Security Emergency"

Sec. 102. (a) In the event of any one of the following:

(1) Invasion of the territory of the United States or its possessions,

(2) Declaration of war by Congress, or

(3) Insurrection within the United States in aid of a foreign enemy,

and if, upon the occurrence of one or more of the above, the President shall find that the proclamation of an emergency pursuant to this section is essential to the preservation, protection and defense of the Constitution, and to the common defense and safety of the territory and people of the United States, the President is authorized to make public proclamation of the existence of an "Internal Security Emergency".

(b) A state of "Internal Security Emergency" (hereinafter referred to as the "emergency") so declared shall continue in existence until terminated by proclamation of the President or by concurrent resolution of the Congress.

Detention During Emergency

Sec. 103. (a) Whenever there shall be in existence such an emergency, the President, acting through the Attorney General, is hereby authorized to apprehend and by order detain, pursuant to the provisions of this title, each person as to whom there is reasonable ground to believe that such person probably will engage in, or probably will conspire with others to engage in, acts of espionage or of sabotage. . . .

17

Repeal of the Emergency Detention Act of 1950: The "Unfounded" Fears of Americans

Document 17†

December 2, 1969

Honorable James O. Eastland
Chairman, Committee on the Judiciary
United States Senate
Washington, D.C. 20510

Dear Senator:

This is in response to your request for the views of the Department of Justice on S. 1872, legislation to repeal the Emergency Detention Act of 1950.

The Emergency Detention Act was enacted as Title II of the Internal Security Act of 1950. In brief, the Act established procedures for the apprehension and detention, during internal security emergencies, of individuals likely to engage in acts of espionage or sabotage.

Unfortunately, the legislation has aroused among many of the citizens of the United States the belief that it may one day be used to accomplish the apprehension and detention of citizens who hold unpopular beliefs and views. In addition, various groups, of which our Japanese-American citizens are most prominent, look upon the legislation as permitting a reoccurrence of the roundups which resulted in the detention of Americans of Japanese ancestry during World War II. It is therefore quite clear that the continuation of the Emergency Detention Act is extremely offensive to many Americans.

†From: Files of the Department of Justice, Washington, D.C.

In the judgment of this Department, the repeal of this legislation will allay the fears and suspicions—unfounded as they may be—of many of our citizens. This benefit outweighs any potential advantage which the Act may provide in a time of internal security emergency.

Accordingly, the Department of Justice recommends the repeal of the Emergency Detention Act of 1950 as proposed in S. 1872.

The Bureau of the Budget has advised there is no objection to the submission of this report from the standpoint of the Administration's program.

Sincerely,
RICHARD G. KLEINDIENST
Deputy Attorney General

Part three

Bibliographic Note

The bulk of this book is based upon documents stored in the National Archives, Washington, D.C. Dr. Stetson Conn, former chief military historian of the Department of the Army, was the first to exploit most of them and his guidance in tracking them down was invaluable. Other documentation may be found in the Franklin D. Roosevelt papers and the "Diaries" of Henry Morgenthau, Jr., at the Franklin D. Roosevelt Library, Hyde Park; the diaries of Henry M. Stimson at Yale University, the Joseph W. Stilwell Diaries at the Hoover Institution, Stanford University, and in the papers of Culbert Olson at the Bancroft Library, University of California, Berkeley.

The published accounts which treat the decision to evacuate are far too voluminous for a complete listing here: the best bibliographical essay in print is Howard Sugimoto, "A Bibliographical Essay on the Wartime Evacuation of Japanese from the West Coast Areas," pp. 140-150 in H. Conroy and T.S. Miyakawa, eds., *East Across the Pacific: Historical and Sociological Studies of Japanese Immigration and Assimilation* (Santa Barbara, 1972). The major studies that focus on the decision itself are, in chronological order: Carey McWilliams, *Prejudice: Japanese Americans: Symbol of Racial Intolerance* (Boston, 1944); Morton Grodzins, *Americans Betrayed: Politics and the Japanese Evacuation* (Chicago, 1949); Jacobus tenBroek, Edward N. Barnhart, and Floyd W. Matson, *Prejudice, War, and the Constitution* (Berkeley and Los Angeles, 1954); Stetson Conn, "Japanese Evacuation from the West Coast," pp. 115-49 in *The United States Army in World War II: The Western Hemisphere: Guarding the United States and Its Outposts*, eds. Stetson Conn, Rose C. Engleman, and Byron Fairchild, (Washington, 1964); Allan R. Bosworth, *America's Concentration Camps* (New York, 1967); Bill Hosokawa, *Nisei: The Quiet Americans* (New York, 1969); Audrie Girdner and Anne Loftis, *The Great Betrayal* (New York, 1969); and Roger Daniels, *Concentration Camps, U.S.A.: Japanese Americans and World War II* (New York, 1971).

A topic not explored in the present work is the impact of the relocation on the Japanese Americans who were its victims. Harry H.L. Kitano, *Japanese Americans: The Evolution of a Subculture* (Englewood Cliffs, N.J., 1969), is an analysis by a scholar who was graduated from high school in the Topaz (Central Utah) camp. Memoir accounts by victims include: Mine Okubo, *Citizen 12660* (New York, 1946); Monica Sone, *Nisei Daughter* (Boston, 1953); Daisuke Kitagawa, *Issei and Nisei: The Internment Years* (New York, 1967); Sue K. Embrey, ed., *The Lost Years, 1942-1946* (Los Angeles, 1972); Estelle Ishigo, *Lone Heart Mountain* (Los Angeles, 1972); and Jeanne Wakatsuki Houston and James Houston, *Farewell to Manzanar* (Boston, 1973). There are superb photographs in Masie and Richard Conrat, *Executive Order 9066* (Los Angeles, 1972). A historiographic treatment of the entire Asian American experience may be found in Roger Daniels, "American Historians and East Asian Immigrants," *Pacific Historical Review* (No., 1974).